"... TALLY ... VOLUNT[...]
BUTZ WHERE THERE W[...]
VEST CROPS ... YORAM, SLEEPLESS, VOLUNTEERED
FOR EVERYTHING WITHIN SIGHT ... SCHOOLCHIL-
DREN SANDBAGGED DOORS AND DUG TRENCHES
AT THE KINDERGARTEN ... NAOMI DID AIR RAID
DRILLS AND PLAYED IN THE SHELTER WHERE I
READ *WINNIE-THE-POOH* ..."

IN THE MIDST OF WAR—
A LETTER FROM ISRAEL

The quotation above is taken from a letter written to the
Editorial Director of Bantam Books from a friend in Israel.
The full text of this extraordinarily moving letter is reprinted
here:

9 June 1967
(The 5th Day of War)
10:00 a.m.

Your cable came yesterday. I can't tell you, without an
overflow of what might seem like sentimentality, how very
touched and grateful we were.

THESE HAVE BEEN MOST ASTONISHING TIMES.
The two weeks of dreadful tension when all of us faced what
we thought might, quite literally, be extermination, and the
death of the young State, and our own total abandonment by
the world. And then, the four breathless, incredible days and
heights of victory.

I WONDER IF EVER BEFORE A COUNTRY HAS
FOUGHT WITH SUCH BRILLIANCE AND VALOR AND
DETERMINATION—so rapidly and so successfully. Everyone stood the test, to perfection. The new immigrants, the
oldtimers, the people who have lived through so much before
and might have been forgiven for failing to muster strength
and nerve. But truly no one failed. No one at all.

AS I WRITE, THE NEWS OF THE CEASE FIRE COMES
HURTLING OVER THE RADIO. It is all so extraordinary
and we are all elated, though weary and worn by the strain and
the worry and the fact that the casualty lists are not all in yet.

BUT THE COUNTRY IS OURS, AND THE BORDERS ARE SECURE AND JERUSALEM IS ONE AGAIN. I can hardly grasp the extent of triumph. Now, we must work towards lasting peace so that this will never happen again, not to us and not to our neighbors.

THE CHILDREN WERE WONDERFUL. Tally plugged away, palely, at working for her finals, and volunteered at a nearby kibbutz where there were no men left to harvest crops, and was very frightened each time the air raid alarms sounded but very quiet and very disciplined. Yoram, sleepless, volunteered for everything within sight. School barely functioned and the schoolchildren sandbagged doors and dug trenches at the kindergarden and worked as messengers and stood guard. Naomi did air raid drills and played in the shelter where I read *Winnie-the-Pooh* (yet) and told her that it would be all right long before I believed it myself. But she only cried once at night, and quite understood that one must behave properly.

Perhaps I should have waited to write you a more coherent letter but I wanted you to hear from us at once and know that WE ARE WELL AND JUBILANT AND TERRIBLY PROUD of the wonderful army that delivered us in such a spectacular, marvelous way. They are for us what the RAF was for Britain—and then some. And you should see them—so beautiful, and so brave, and so ordinary. With the least swagger possible.

I WISH YOU HAD BEEN HERE, in a way. But now why don't you do a quick book? Like the others. Correspondents' stories and photos and perhaps a lot of stuff from the local press and local cartoons and radio material . . .

IT WOULD BE FINE TO HAVE A PRINTED SOUVENIR of "His Terrible Swift Sword." It is, you know, as though Jehovah stands by His own people only when they are on their own soil. I even feel, today when one can permit oneself to write and say things which otherwise are taboo, that perhaps back of the Israel Defense Forces there stood the shadow army of six million Jews who could neither fight nor win.

WELL, WE SHALL TALK ABOUT ALL THIS SOME OTHER TIME. When you are back here, or we are in New York. Do write. I am anxious to know how you fare. And do think about doing a book. If I can help, of course I will.

Much love, and forgive this ill-typed and confused note.

As ever,
Rinna

A BOOK FOR RINNA AND
TALLY AND NAOMI AND YORAM . . .

We have published the book. It was rushed into print at a pace almost as extraordinary as the war itself. STRIKE ZION! is a unique book in several aspects. Like Rinna, many people offered to help in its creation. One, William Stevenson, novelist and an editor with CBC-TV's weekly documentary series, *Newsmagazine,* had been in Israel one week before the outbreak of hostilities.

CHOOSING AN AUTHOR

William Stevenson is the internationally-renowned journalist who, on the eve of the Suez crisis, reported an exclusive story that made front-page headlines throughout the world. He had followed a series of clues that led to Cairo, and the discovery that Dr. Johannes von Leers, an escaped Nazi war criminal, was working for the UAR as chief of Egypt's anti-Israeli broadcasts.

Stevenson found von Leers, interviewed him, reported the story and, after a period of imprisonment, was expelled from Egypt.

Having covered every major conflict in the world since World War II, Bill Stevenson now wanted to do a book on the incredible six-day Israeli campaign.

MAN ON THE SCENE

A week before the actual fighting began, Stevenson—in Israel—knew that war was inevitable. He had talked with hundreds of Israeli citizens and high government officials. On the streets and in the pubs where the press gathered, he watched the tension build. All during the lightning mobilization, he was the man on the scene.

To gather a more complete picture of the political climate behind the war, Stevenson alternated flying between the United States, Canada and Israel. He reported and commented on United Nations activity. He had been in Moscow when the Mideast crisis began to brew, and was one of the few men able to put into perspective Russia's strange role in the war.

William Stevenson—by virtue of his background, his current involvement, his writing skill and his interest—was, of course, the man to write the book.

THE AUTHOR OF EXODUS

Leon Uris arrived in New York during the time that Bantam was confirming plans with Stevenson. Uris, whose novel on the struggle to create Israel—*Exodus*—has sold well over twenty million copies, was deeply concerned about the war.

He offered a magnificent addition to the book—an exclusive special section describing Israel's unique history and heritage, and a fascinating insight into what the six-day war has accomplished. "Things will never be the same again," Uris contends. And in STRIKE ZION! he explains why.

FROM BANTAM—FOR RINNA . . .

From its conception to its completion, STRIKE ZION! represents one of the most exciting projects Bantam Books has ever initiated.

It was motivated by the desire to present a comprehensive account; to tie together the bits and pieces of information that deluged, and often confused, newspaper readers; to fill in the details that strict censorship during the war suppressed; to relate the little stories, the true tales of heroism, and even humor in the midst of a desperate battle for survival. And to answer the public's cry for the full story *NOW*.

For Rinna—for everyone—here is "the printed souvenir."

STRIKE ZION!

STRIKE ZION!

BY WILLIAM STEVENSON

WITH A SPECIAL SECTION
BY LEON URIS

MAPS AND A 64-PAGE
PORTFOLIO OF PHOTOGRAPHS

STRIKE ZION!
A Bantam Book / published July 1967

Published simultaneously in the United States and Canada

Bantam Books are published by Bantam Books, Inc., a subsidiary
of Grosset & Dunlap, Inc. Its trade-mark, consisting of the words
"Bantam Books" and the portrayal of a bantam, is registered in the
United States Patent Office and in other countries. Marca Registrada.
Bantam Books, Inc., 271 Madison Avenue, New York, N.Y. 10016.

PRINTED IN THE UNITED STATES OF AMERICA

CONTENTS

Captions and acknowledgments for
photographs appear on page 143.

Part I: Prelude

CHAPTER ONE

The clocks stopped in Israel on Monday, June 5, 1967, and they started again a week later. That's how most people felt. For instance a gathering of generals on the evening of June 12 was disrupted somewhat by the question: "When exactly did you reach the Suez Canal?" Some said Wednesday and some said Thursday but the fact was that they, like every citizen, regarded that week as something outside of time as we know it. For one thing, as marked on military calendars, they formed the beginning of a countdown: 10 days–9–8–7–6–5–4–3–2–1. At Day Zero, if Israel's carefully hoarded jets and tanks had failed decisively to vanquish the Egyptians, the tide would have turned against them. The inescapable logic of dwindling fuel reserves and the narrow margin of combat effectiveness would have made disaster certain, had the enemy known how to delay by even a few hours the long-range spears of armor.

"We *might* have had a few days in hand," confessed a strategist operating one of the computers employed during the week of desert battles. "But the sheer weight of Arab numbers and arms would have swung against us by the second week."

It is doubtful if the rest of the world yet understands just what a Goliath confronted David. The war was over so quickly. It seemed, to one TV critic watching the battle films, "like a John Wayne movie." You had to smell the corpses thick as flies along the paths of war. You had to see the crushed Russian-built jets and the melancholy Russian-built tanks with guns drooping as they lay abandoned or gutted. You had to read the casualty lists in the *Jerusalem Post* with their disproportionate number of dead majors and colonels. You had to examine the Russian SA–2 missile base, the first to be captured intact anywhere. You had to fly over the 25 Arab airbases where warplanes lay squashed like moths in the sand,

1

and see the antlike armies of disarmed Arabs staggering home across the sandy wastes. You had to see the tension in Jewish faces, so carefully disguised (and who ever said a stiff upper lip was an Anglo-Saxon monopoly?). You had to be in the foreign correspondents' favorite Tel Aviv hangout, The Dan's grill room, and hear the head of the Weizmann Institute, Meier Weisgel, with his prophetlike profile and his flying wings of gray hair, say, "Today the Jews are standing straight." You had to see the barboy back at work in his brown-and-green desert fatigues, unconcerned after 72 hours behind a 105-mm mounted on a Centurion tank that fought its way through a stubborn Egyptian rearguard action. You had to read an Irish-Catholic's dispatch to his London newspaper: "Today I'm a little ashamed not to be Jewish."

Most foreigners in Tel Aviv shared his unease that Israel fought alone. Certainly it was with a sense of helpless disgust that I came here from an endless and indecisive debate in the UN Security Council that followed the abruptly ordered withdrawal of the UN peacekeeping force from Egypt. Its immediate consequence was President Gamal Abdel Nasser's claim to hold against all comers the Strait of Tiran—that narrow opening to the Gulf of Aqaba. The Gulf is a 100-mile waterway running along the Sinai Peninsula to Israel's new port of Elath and to Jordan's only port of Aqaba.

The Strait had been excluded from the slow-simmering crisis that seemed always to be approaching boiling point after the Suez operation of 1956. That year the Sinai campaign enabled the Israelis to force open the strait and establish Elath as a gateway to trade in Asia and Africa. Then, for reasons that may have had everything to do with an aging dictator's need for new external triumphs, Nasser staked his reputation as leader of the Arab revolution. On Monday May 22 he plugged the narrow outlet which provided Israel with an alternative route to the Suez Canal, already closed to her shipping.

Even an observer at the UN with no emotional commitments could see that Israel would get little sympathy or help from that quarter. What none of us knew, as outsiders, was that some of Israel's leaders were coming slowly and reluctantly to the conclusion that their Arab enemies were speeding up their so-called "salami tactics." The slicing away of Israel's brief and hard-won independence approached the rapidity of a buzzsaw.

At what point should the victim stand firm? Each slice from the sausage could appear, in the cool detached atmosphere of the UN, to be unworthy of panic. The Russians at the UN protested against the calling of an emergency session of the Security Council to discuss Egypt's latest moves. There was, they said, no emergency. Israel saw some of her friends waver and, in the case of France, even make expedient moves to the Arab side.

There were, meanwhile, indications that Nasser was closing in for a kill. Israel felt strangled by the tightening ring of Arab armor. She had enough arms and men to stand a fair chance of breaking this stranglehold, but the risks were enormous. Suppose the Russians intervened? Suppose a preventive war lasted longer than Israel's limited resources could endure? Defense Minister Moshe Dayan scented trouble and asked to visit forces in the desert.

The gamble was that of a people who knew, by some deep mysterious instinct that defies analysis, that the time had come for action. You felt this gathering resolve in the days immediately before the war. Children filled sandbags, with a curious kind of calm resignation. Old air-raid shelters were emptied of their accumulated rubbish, so that street corners were suddenly littered with broken furniture and mildewed trunks and all the bric-a-brac of quiet suburban life. Mothers baked bread and fathers on civil-defense duties slept in classrooms and museums. So many cakes were being mailed to the desert units that the army was obliged to plead for a halt to the avalanche of goodies. Taxis disappeared from the road as the drivers were mobilized. The Sheraton Hotel, overlooking the golden beaches of Tel Aviv, was stripped for use as a casualty station. Storm lanterns appeared in the corridors of the massive Hilton; and day by day, the dwindling number of guests moved downward from floor to floor as rooms were closed and the basement reinforced. "I felt we were making a slow descent," said a volunteer Canadian doctor, "into hell."

A bizarre scene that seemed to dramatize this new mood was enacted early one morning when a mobile blood bank raided Mandy's Discotheque. This was the celebrated Mandy Rice-Davies, the London blonde swinger who figured in the Profumo scandal that rocked the British establishment. In Tel Aviv she became a young matron of consequence, but the crisis broke while she was away. "If Mandy doesn't return," said her clients, "it will be the ruin of her discotheque." She did return in a burst of publicity. (MANDY GOES TO FIGHT FOR ISRAEL was one exuberant and premature headline in London.)

3

Four days before the war actually started, doctors and nurses raided her establishment in a basement under Tel Aviv's main drag. Young playboys and their go-go girl friends were laid out on chairs and blood was drawn from their unusually limp arms. "Aren't you worried about alcohol content?" I asked a young doctor. "Hell no!" he said cheerfully. "They're too—er, *weak* to resist and I'd rather have a few quarts of whisky-flavored plasma than none at all."

The blood, as it turned out, was badly needed a week later when the casualties began to pour back from the nearby desert battles.

It seemed as if everyone knew in his bones that the die was already cast, although no formal decision had been taken. A dovelike cabinet took into its ranks a couple of so-called hawks, although the parallel with U.S. doves and hawks is misleading since this was a country with its back to the wall, and all parties were closing ranks. General Moshe Dayan, the 52-year-old hero of the Sinai campaign which he directed, became Minister of National Defense; and Menahem Begin, once the elusive leader of the underground terrorist Irgun Zvai Leumi, became a Minister Without Portfolio. Both men, talking on the eve of war, conveyed the same sense of cold resolve. I had heard they were extremists. They seemed to be men who saw only too clearly that Israel would cease to exist if she turned away from the Arab challenge yet again.

General Dayan was often accused of a swashbuckling, swaggering manner. His black patch over one eye (the left) was said by countrymen who were critical of him to be pure melodrama. The truth was that he lost an eye fighting with the British in Syria in 1941 and plastic surgeons said regretfully that extensive damage to the muscle tissue around the socket made it impossible to fit him with a glass eye. The scar under the patch (if scar is the right word for that kind of mutilation) was not pretty. He was a 52-year-old farmer, a great believer in collective farming, who tackled Israel's problems with typical military forthrightness when he was Minister of Agriculture and produced among other things a tomato known as "the moneymaker" which he said would earn his country vast sums in foreign exchange. Like some of his other ideas, this one fell a long way short of its promise; but at least he tried. He had a relaxed charm and an inquisitive mind (he developed a passion for archeology and "digs") and for this, he was forgiven much.

4

Begin was another case altogether. After the assassination of Abraham Stern, the leader of the Stern Gang, he was the most wanted man by British security forces, although he opposed Stern's terrorist methods. It was that unhappy period when Britain, given a League of Nations mandate over Palestine, banned the immigration of Jews. His Herut Party was associated with the demand for a single undivided Israel on both sides of the Jordan, and General Dayan and other so-called "hawks" were in fact dubious about an expanded state which might only seem to confirm Arab fears.

Behind such men was the arch exponent of blitzkrieg: that crusty 82-year-old fighter David Ben-Gurion. "Our soldiers," he had said, "don't lead from behind. That's what makes our army different." He argued, as he always had, that Jews must heed the lessons of history. They could not rely on the gentile world for support in times of crisis. The Arabs would never abandon their plans for Israel's total destruction until they were given a massive and decisive demonstration of Jewish courage and strength. "Depend," he said, "upon our own right arm and nobody else's."

This sentiment found an echo in General Dayan's first press conference after he was coopted as defense minister. War was 36 hours away. "I don't want American or British boys to get killed here," he said. "I don't think we need outside help."

In retrospect, General Dayan's exuberance seemed hard to understand; his confidence appeared almost suicidal. His tiny country, about the size of Massachusetts, thrust like a dagger into the Arab world. His less than 3 million people were confronted by 14 Arab nations. If numbers and propaganda meant anything, he faced the implacable hatred of 110 million Arabs. His intelligence organs (whose members enjoyed the enormous advantage of speaking Arabic, whereas few Arabs spoke Hebrew) had assembled facts and figures that confirmed a frightening superiority in Arab war materiel. Israel's tanks and jets, for instance, were obsolescent. Egypt and Syria alone were equipped with the latest weapons for desert and air warfare including ground-to-air missiles first tested in action around Hanoi.

Whatever the odds against Israel, and they were so formidable that even now an outsider is haunted by a sense of astonishment that Tel Aviv still stands, the mood of the country had hardened to one of calm resolve.

A sense of avenging the past was strong. And the feel-

5

ing of unfinished business was everywhere. There had been too many unpunished shellings of border settlements, too many attempts to choke the shipping and air lanes to the east, too many Nazilike threats. "How horrifying," said Lord Avon, the former Anthony Eden, "that it should be thought a godly deed by Arabs to butcher a whole people or call by [Cairo] radio for genocide, yet that is what is happening."

In Tel Aviv the affluent had for a long time bought TV sets although Israel had no television itself. So they watched Cairo instead. Their screens were filled with the hysterical abuse of Nasser's puppets. Fists waved against the Jews. Martial parades goose-stepped toward a holy war. "It was so hypnotic," said Captain Amos Sapir, son of the finance minister, "you found yourself nodding your head as someone said what a lousy lot we were." Amos, a paratroop reservist, had come back from four years in New York to help his country. He was injured and a companion, one of my colleagues, killed a few days later. Hardly anyone escaped the brush of violent death. To outsiders the war might have seemed swift and neat as a surgeon's knife. An entire week was lifted out of the calendar like an ugly cancer. Only those who took part, and that meant almost every Israeli adult, knew how dirty it really was.

A decision to operate had been taken already by Friday, May 26, when Israel's armies drew tight the bowstrings and Israel's air force quivered in the slips. There was too much menace in the Egyptian movement of five infantry divisions and two armored divisions into the Sinai which had been a wilderness between the two nations, an empty desert that gave support to those who said Egypt was not serious in claiming a state of war had always existed. Eighty thousand Egyptian troops and 900 Russian-built tanks, and Russian-built missiles and giant rockets were pointing at Israel, and from the opposite flank came Jordan's renewed threat of holy war, and the appearance in Syria of Russian military advisors. An Egyptian strike force of 200 tanks moved upon Elath, Israel's outlet to East Africa and Asia. The shadow of approaching peril fell upon Israel and her leaders were resigned to facing danger alone.

"We'd lost confidence in the intellectual chat of world statesmen," said a military commander. "They shirked action and we saw the issues being lost in another UN debate while

Nasser drew the noose and waited to see if any power would stop him from pulling it yet tighter."

A suspicion swept through Israel that some political leaders, scholars by nature and easygoing in the East European way, would be reluctant to act, would continue to hope Nasser had no evil intent despite Egyptian abuse, despite the transfer of some of his forces from Yemen to the borders of Israel, despite the expulsion of UN peacekeepers, the blocking of a vital waterway, and the conclusion of an encircling military pact.

"Strike first!" argued the military commanders, knowing how each day whittled down their strength. Premier Levi Eshkol's coalition government still hesitated. His Foreign Minister, Abba Eban, was in Washington listening to American doubts. On that same Friday, May 26, when Israel's desert commanders were actually in possession of first-strike orders, and the assault jets were loaded with secret 12-foot guided bombs, the word got out that Israel was about to pounce on the grounds that in this opposition of two tense armies, the first to punch would win. Urgent messages were delivered to both sides from Washington and Moscow. The Egyptians were asked by President Johnson (so Nasser stated later) not to fire first: and at 3:30 A.M., the Soviet ambassador in Cairo, Dmitri Pojidaev, called on Nasser with a similar appeal.

Eban, the Israeli Foreign Minister, was booked on TWA's Flight 5404 due to depart Kennedy at 10:15 P.M. to Tel Aviv via Rome. The Boeing–707 waited 30 minutes before the captain decided that further delay was unwarranted.

"We've just had word that highway traffic is holding up the Israeli Prime Minister," he said. (Several passengers looked startled, knowing Premier Eshkol to be in Israel, but Eban was avoiding publicity and the airline's staff knew him only as a statesman of some consequence. The Mideast crisis had not yet thrust Israel into the same prominence as Vietnam and there was a forgivable confusion about personalities.) Later, free drinks were served to mollify the other passengers. There was a small burst of applause for TWA's generosity from American tourists already in holiday mood. *They* were getting off at Rome.

There was less applause in Tel Aviv. The report spread swiftly that President Johnson, alarmed by U.S. intelligence digests from the scene, recalled Eban at the last moment and thus made him miss the plane. He informed Eban that if Israel's armies moved at this critical juncture they might (in-

7

deed, almost certainly would) lose the sympathy of the Western world. There might well be a repetition of the events of 1956 when Israel reacted powerfully to Egyptian provocation, and found herself suddenly and inexplicably condemned for seizing the Sinai Peninsula and inflicting an embarrassing defeat on Nasser. Then as now, said the U.S. President, it was no use Israel asserting that Egypt made the first move. The public's memory was short and many people would condemn Israel as a militant nation, only too ready to grab extra territory. He asked Israel to postpone action.

Eban, a persuasive man with a Churchillian manner and a quick brain, pointed out that if Israel continued to maintain its present defensive posture in the face of Arab pressures, she would go bankrupt. The whole country was an armed camp. It had to be, so long as Nasser's propaganda machine proclaimed daily the Arab intention to destroy Israel. There were documents, said Eban, to show that Egypt planned to annihilate the Jews. In these circumstances Israel must keep up its guard, but the cost was enormous.

In Tel Aviv the rumor spread that President Johnson then offered to underwrite the cost of mobilization to the tune of $3 million a day. This was certainly the understanding of professional soldiers who form an establishment of their own in Israel, and General Dayan was asked if he wanted to see the country dependent on U.S. whims and fancies.

He did not. One of his aides pointed out that Washington would be busy with its sums: "There's no oil in Israel, but on the other hand there are no Arab voters in America." In other words, what was more important: Arab oil or the Jewish vote? This cynical question went down badly with men born and raised on the kitbutzim, those collectives where idealism took the place of money-grubbing, where self-help and manual labor had created a new kind of individual unaccustomed to go cap-in-hand for help.

General Dayan was a man from the kibbutz and so were his commanders. They believed Arab guns were cocked. They had no doubt about Arab intentions, which were confirmed by documents captured in a variety of ways, not all likely to meet with UN approval.

"When," asked General Abraham Yoffe, "does a strike become preemptive?" And that was the whole point. Both sides were shivering like hounds on the leash. The first to slip free would make the kill. General Yoffe was not the kind of man to

8

seek trouble. Indeed his normal occupation was the protection of wildlife. He had lectured a few days earlier on the preservation of game and certain species of orchid which ought not to be picked because they were rare. He commanded the reserves and when it became clear that Israel had better rely upon her own limited strength, he set into motion the next few stages of mobilization.

The code words were broadcast every half hour on the fateful Monday of June 5: "Lovers of Zion"/"The Wedding March"/"Past and Future"/"Peace and Greetings"/"The Last of the Just"/"Deep Roots"/"Close Shave"/"Limelight"/"Bitter Rice"/"Open Window"/"Field of Gold" and perhaps most apt of all, in view of the enemy's noisy boasting threats, "Bullfighters." The overall campaign was later to be called "Strike Zion."

General Dayan made his first and last appearance as the prewar Defense Minister on the preceding Saturday: "We have seen," he said, "the collapse of arrangements made ten, eleven years ago through international organs . . . if diplomacy achieves freedom of passage through the Straits of Tiran I will be very glad."

It was evident he had lost any remaining faith in the ability of the UN or friendly governments to avert the danger. "I do not want or expect people to fight and get killed for us," he said.

Within the next 40 hours, the final decision was taken. Almost all the remaining stages of mobilization were launched. Only one code name remained and that would have amounted to a cry of despair. It was based upon the assumption that Israel's forces might fail to smash the enemy in the first moment of surprise. It was called *"Mikre Hakol"* or "Situation Everyone," and it meant that every Jew, of whatever age or sex, would fight to the death.

The citizens of Tel Aviv, now torn between their civilian occupations and the significance of their reservist uniforms, heard the whine of jets that Monday morning at the hour when shops and offices open. Needle-nosed tactical bombers lifted off from nearby airbases, many of them unknown to the local people, and swung out across the Mediterranean with slender 12-foot bombs under each clipped wing.

In a ground-floor Tel Aviv apartment, used by the Irgun underground fighters in the 1948 "War of Independence" and still a meeting place for the tough survivors of Nazi extermination camps, someone found the Hebrew Bible belonging to Menahem Begin, the new Minister Without Portfolio who had

9

kept the underground veterans together. Begin was once a rabbi and the Bible was open at the 20th chapter of Deuteronomy:

When thou goest into battle against thine enemies,
and seest horses, and chariots, and a people more than
thou, be not afraid: for the Lord thy God is with thee,
which brought thee up out of the land of Egypt . . . Hear
O Israel: . . . let not your hearts be faint, fear not,
and do not tremble.

A letter arrived in London from Yael Dayan, the 28-year-old daughter of General Dayan. Like so many other Israeli adults, she was now a soldier. She wrote:

You should see me now. High boots, white with dust,
khaki uniform, canteen and knife in belt, and a wide-
brimmed desert hat. My skin is brown-black and smothered
with dust—*and I don't think I ever felt better.*
The Egyptian trenches are within sight and our soldiers
are in touch and the border is like a question mark . . .
Everywhere is white dust: sandstorms turn the dust into
whirlpools in the air which mould scenery and the faces into
one large screen of yellow . . . Waiting is harder than war.
Like a spring ready to go, a trigger left unpressed, the whole
machine is tense and expectant.

Thousands of women knew the feeling. They were part of a people's army without parallel or precedent. They were about to take part in a war which would set new records—the biggest tank battle in history, the most successful employment of limited air power, the swiftest of victories.

A week later General Dayan stood at the Wailing Wall in the Old City of Jerusalem, in the presence of all his army commanders whose military titles have biblical sources, and said:

We have liberated the Temple area, broken through the
blockade of our seas and captured the heights overlooking
our villages in Galilee and the Jordan Valley.
The Arab armies which set out to conquer us now lie at
our feet. From Sharm el Sheikh in southern Sinai to El
Quneitra in Syria lie the remnants of tanks, planes, and
cannon, smoking skeletons and scrap metal left behind by
the armies of Egypt, Syria, and Jordan which attempted
to wipe the State of Israel from the map.
We have defeated the enemy. We have crushed his forces

10

and frustrated his plots. The price is heavy. The best of our comrades, the bravest of our fighters, the dearest of our sons have fallen in action. The sands of the desert and the rocks of Galilee are drenched with their blood.

An air hostess on El Al's first flight to leave New York since the start of hostilities, Flight 272, collapsed. When she left Tel Aviv her country was at peace, her fiancé making plans for an early wedding. Now he was dead, his transsonic Mystère a pile of rubble in the sand. And Israel was again at peace. A week had passed but not every week has seven days.

CHAPTER TWO

*Letter by the author to a Jewish friend
on Saturday, June 3, 1967, two days before the war*

TEL AVIV

I'm bewildered and elated and just a bit frightened for the Jews. It feels exactly the way it did when I was a schoolboy in London just before the Nazis began to bomb. Everyone's gentle and cheerful, and there's no sign of panic—except, I'm told, among a few who've heard the Egyptians will use gas.

It's like watching the lights dim in a theater. Exactly the same, because the lights *have* been going out, bit by bit. We arrived last week. Each night since, the public lighting system has been a bit more curtailed. The enormous department store Kol-Bo Shalom, which sticks up like a sore thumb in the eastern end of the Mediterranean, is blacked out. People say this way, the Egyptian bombers will fly into it.

"Shalom!" What a lovely greeting this is. You know what it means; but remember I'm new here, new to your people for that matter. When I heard what it meant I felt a sudden surge of compassion for any nation that can live in the shadow of destruction and say at every opportunity: *Shalom! Peace!* They say it to you in shops, on the switchboard, just catching your eye in the street. There must be a very deep thirst for peace in a country built partly from human bits and pieces left by Europe's wars. To be honest, knowing what this country is probably in for, I feel my eyes prick when I hear it: *Shalom!*

All week the men and girls have been disappearing from the streets, almost furtively, age-group by group. Nobody *says* anything. It's weird, if you're a stranger. You expect bands and a lot of jingoistic blah. But here they slip away to war—I hope it *isn't* war, but I fear it is—without any fuss, in accord-

12

ance with a mobilization plan that seems brilliant. My taxi driver said today he couldn't come back for me after lunch because he got his call-up, waiting for me. I said how? He pointed to the radio. "Our units have code signs." He drives a tank now.

The big doorman at the hotel vanished today too. He told me the Egyptians were no sweat, they did everything by the book. He goes ahead of the main column with a mine detector. He said when he finds a mine, he knows where the others will probably be, because "they" follow the same pattern of mine-laying every time.

War definitely is expected. Each day we see another subtle change. First it was the old air-raid shelters being emptied out, the rubbish appearing on the streets. Then the shop windows were crisscrossed with tape against blast. Suddenly children are delivering the mail. All the tourists have been slowly melting away. My hotel is nearly empty—imagine 18 empty floors on the Mediterranean! DANCE IN THE EXOTIC AT-MOSPHERE OF A BEDOUIN TENT, says a card in my room. KING SOLOMON'S GRILL. Now, there's nobody to dance with. And no waiter to open the grill.

We drove south of Beersheba today to one of the armored brigades poised opposite Egyptian divisions from Yemen. The colonel was indifferent at first. Then he got interested in the cameras, and suddenly he was laying on a Lawrence of Arabia movie for us. We couldn't have *hired* something like it. He wouldn't give his name because he doesn't want terrorist reprisals against his kids. I suddenly understood why he was so cool. He'd been waiting there for a week for the order to slam into the Egyptians.

The desert was bare when we arrived. We had a hard time finding the command vehicles. Everything was camouflaged. There was a cold efficiency about the equipment—no spit and polish, and no pretense about shining the brass knobs, but a deadly underlying efficiency. Moses, the liaison officer, said it was up to the colonel if he wanted to cooperate. I must have looked skeptical because he added: "In this army, the field commanders are their own bosses."

The colonel asked what we needed. I said could he raise a little action? Ten minutes later the desert came alive with half-tracks and infantry breaking out of camouflage. I spent my wars mostly at sea and this was like watching a fleet come out of the mist. The vehicles moved under clouds of sand. Two

13

Mystère jets dropped like bolts out of the sky and Colonel X looked very smug but pretended he knew nothing about it. He's a lot smarter than he looks at first, and by the end of the day I was impressed by what he had *not* revealed to us, although he never once dodged a question or made an obvious attempt to conceal anything.

This secretiveness is not normal. People here are open and friendly. And yet they're in the habit of protecting their small land from surrounding enemies, and you become aware of being shut out from some things—like the disposition of kibbutz guns. You must get this way after twenty years of being shelled by an enemy you can't punish, having your roads and bridges blown up by fanatics.

One of the girls with the brigade, one of ten girls attached to this unit, said she was born on a kibbutz and would go back when she finishes army service. I asked why, which must have sounded stupid, because she laughed and said she couldn't imagine any other kind of life. "You work for each other," she said, "and money doesn't mean anything." She explained her army duties and I suddenly realized this child would be riding in the lead half-track with Colonel X into the Egyptian guns. She ran the half-track like the bridge of a destroyer: charts and binoculars neatly stowed, radiophones strapped in place, clipboards marked up, wax pencils ready. She was very quick and unobtrusive, like a squirrel, but she had an odd kind of authority and the men obviously respected her. She had the authority of someone who knows exactly what she's doing and why, and something in her quiet and remote gaze reminded me of the old story about the martyr on Mount Sinai.

Colonel X agreed we should film the men singing around a fire in the night. It sounded Boy Scoutish and I wasn't sure the footage would be good television. About eight, the rest of the crew and myself were stumbling around the desert, shouting for Moses to guide us. It was funny hearing Ed shout "Hey, Moses!" The soldiers move like night animals, surefooted and soundless.

Suddenly several hundred troops came out of the darkness without warning. Floodlamps came on. Colonel X had brought up an entire entertainment team from army headquarters. I swear I never heard them arrive. Just about now it became apparent that nothing was good enough for this brigade, and I had the prickly feeling one gets before trouble. These troops *knew* they were going to war. They squatted in a circle with their officers, and you had to look hard to distinguish the colonel from his men. This really is a citizens' army. They laughed a lot, and sang a lot, and then an entire orchestra infiltrated into the center of the circle. There were a couple of dozen instruments and the conductor was a leading Israeli musician who'd gotten into battledress, and the soloist was Ivry Gitlis, the violinist. Gitlis had walked out of a studio in Paris in the middle of a recording and caught the next plane here. He'd had that same instinct about war coming.

How they navigated a full orchestra to an armored brigade God knows, all the way from Tel Aviv to the middle of the Negev. I couldn't imagine it happening in anyone else's army. No ballyhoo. An hour of good music and then they packed and got into their army buses and rumbled away. Later the men lit an enormous fire and sang very personal songs like "Sands of the Negev," sad and haunting, and I was surprised and moved to see the faces of the girl soldiers in the firelight. They were all crying.

We filmed a lot of interviews with politicians and members of the community. People like to talk when the cameras aren't rolling. I was impressed by their loyalty. Men I'd been told were normally critical of the government or who were bitterly opposed to each other, wouldn't reveal any differences in this time of danger. It was a small thing by which to judge an entire society. I find myself very buoyed up by these people. They don't boast and they're not frightened, and they know exactly why they're likely to be at war next week.

Gas masks are being bought in West Germany. What an incredible irony! The Israeli government is concerned about Egyptian poison-gas wagons and bombs reported to be stored on this side of Suez.

We filmed a large school at air-raid drill this afternoon. Men were digging trenches across the playground. A swarthy old fellow leaned his spade against a mound of earth and folded his bronzed arms on the handle. "Looks like a grave, doesn't it?" He was French, and under the tan on his left forearm I saw his concentration-camp number tattooed.

The children were very solemn and disciplined when the alarm sounded. There was no jostling and fooling around. They'd been prepared for it a long time and they went through the drill sensibly and swiftly. Inside the school I looked at the

15

notice boards and the kids' handiwork: beautifully detailed paintings of birds, wooden models, things I remember from my own schooldays. I felt suddenly sick.

Nothing we've filmed here so far has been arranged. The government information agency helps us get permits, that's all. This says more, to me, than anything else about the kind of country here. In Egypt you can't move for propaganda. It seems strange though that these people, so gifted in their speech and writing, have been unable somehow to convey the urgency of the situation here. You know I came straight from the Security Council. After that performance I think Israel is going to have to do this thing all alone—will have to fight alone, if it comes to it.

The volunteers are flying in, of course. About 3,000 so far. But these are individual decisions, whereas the UN demonstrated how few governments really would get involved if Israel goes to war. At first I thought the atmosphere here was like Dunkirk or the Battle of Britain. But people then were buoyed up with the knowledge of support abroad, and the backing of a vast empire. This reminds me more of Spain. The Spanish Civil War must have been like this, in a way: the clarity of light and the stark landscape and the men and women with a fierce air of independence. The foreign correspondents are piling in, and all of the veterans say the same thing: it's good to be among people whose cause you really can believe in. These are professionals, war correspondents who know their way around. They, at least, are very much committed. I've seen more old friends in the past 24 hours than I've seen since Vietnam, but here you don't have press junkets and so the lesser men are weeded out. A wry Irishman from Radio Eire said tonight he hopes the Israelis don't win too easily. "Because," he said, "my listeners are on their side now . . . so long as they're the underdogs."

None of the old press hands expect an easy victory. There's a lot of gloomy talk about Nasser's rockets—he's paraded so many through Cairo now that you get the impression he hired the entire German V-2 staff from Peenemünde. But it's also known the Israeli air force has a couple of tricks up its sleeve —especially a guided bomb. The air force seems in superb condition. Its fighter-bombers can squeeze as many as ten strikes into a single day because of the quick ground servicing and turnaround.

Jim Cameron reports a lot of pawky humor among Israelis

16

but he says it's impossible for gentiles to repeat it—partly because this is family stuff, and outsiders would be guilty of bad taste if they tried to hawk it around. I know what he means. The only repeatable stories I've heard are that Nasser is a papyrus tiger; and it took a Moses to lead the way out of Egypt and it'll take another Moses (General Moshe Dayan) to lead the way in again.

General Dayan's conscription as Minister of Defense two days ago was regarded as confirmation the country is ready to launch a preventive war. The fact is the cabinet had its plans ready long ago and Dayan's return is part of the machinery. He talked to the press today and he was diplomatic without being stuffy. It was clear he'd no confidence in UN action; he said so, without spelling it out. He has tremendous charm and he underplays everything. He'd been down to see Ben-Gurion on his farm and apparently there had been some argument about the proper reaction to the latest Egyptian moves: Ben-Gurion less eager for action than Dayan.

This country is fantastically busy just building itself. Looking around, I feel depressed. So much hard work going into reclaiming desert, making parks and forests, and nursing a new Jewish pride. And all this threatened by an enemy the Jews cannot destroy because he's too big, but who can destroy them. The preparations for a bloody encounter seem so irreversible and almost, now, inevitable. The military chesspieces are being arranged on the board. It's difficult to understand that men will die and their work be ruined. Disgust, as a colleague says, is the feeling in a stranger. Disgust that it should be happening all over again, and sorrow. I feel almost afraid to say *"Shalom!"*

CHAPTER THREE

Israel is and always has been a state of war as much as a state of mind. Its native sabras are named after the fruit of the cactus—spiky outside but tender within. For those who believe in miracles, the greatest occurred in the week of June 5 to 12, 1967, a period preceding the religious festival of Tabernacle when the time for miracles is best. There were, claim many Jews, six earlier miracles.

First came the wave of emigration at the end of the nineteenth century. Jewish settlers toiled in malarial swamps and sandy deserts under Turkish rule, and were known as "Children of Death."

Then came the creation of a world Zionist movement. The first congress in 1897 sought a national home in Palestine where, at the time, only 35,000 Jews lived. Twenty years later British Foreign Secretary Arthur James Balfour called for free Jewish immigration to a national home in Palestine. A fourth "miracle" was the adoption and modernization of Hebrew so that Jewish settlers from all over the world could use a single tongue.

The creation of Israel as an independent state on May 15, 1948 (the sixth day of Iyar, the Jewish year 5708) ended 2,000 years of disinheritance. The Jews had been expelled, exiled, and persistently persecuted but they never lost faith in *Eretz Yisroel* and an eventual return.

The sixth miracle was Israel's victory over the Arab League's attempt in 1948 to destroy the new state at birth. Armies of Egypt, Jordan (then called Transjordan), Syria, Lebanon, and Iraq, supported by units from Saudi Arabia, committed what UN Secretary-General Trygve Lie called the "first armed aggression since the end of World War II."

"The Jewish people had to fight unceasingly to keep itself

18

alive," Premier Levi Eshkol said 19 years after the return to Zion. "Hopeful ever of redemption, we labored to return to the land of our fathers and to set foundations for the resurgence of an exiled people. We made our arduous way to the shores of that land and we fought to open the gates to our brethren. We acted from an instinct to save the soul of a people."

Born in violence, Israel has bred a new generation of men and women who stand tall and look the world straight in the eye. This is a newcomer's first impression, and it raises several questions about genetics and environment. The blue-eyed girl corporal I met on the Egyptian front was not untypical. Her father was Moroccan, her mother Romanian, but the girl herself was unmistakably Israeli.

"I want to be on the fighting front," she said, "because I've been a fighter all my life." It seemed a bold claim, coming from a slip of a girl. Her job was "to be with my colonel" and she rode into battle on the half-track he commanded, a vehicle that reminded one of a naval vessel with its charts and guns and crew. Indeed, her particular unit, an armored division, operated like a flotilla of fast motor torpedo boats. Of that, more later. What lingers in my memory now, with the girl and her colonel both dead, is the sense of *quality* she conveyed.

She was born on a kibbutz and she should have been, perhaps, a rather lumpish girl. She loved the land, her land, the land of her collective. Something about her said most emphatically that this girl, and others like her in the same unit, were not there merely to coddle the men. The hot desert winds had fashioned their young faces and the constant making and breaking of camp had molded their taut young bodies. They were not plump little farm girls who might be expected to welcome a roll in the hay. When I asked the corporal what drew her back to the kibbutz she said very simply: "It's one place where people love each other."

She used the word "love" in its widest sense. Any physical implication would have seemed, I am sure, childish. She went on to discuss the atmosphere of love that makes Israel a kind of family-state. She knew all about Tel Aviv's desertion to the ranks of Mediterranean playgrounds. She knew that tourists often saw only the prickly, unfriendly side of her people. "But we're not animals in a zoo," she said, "and for myself I would never waste time trying to please these people who come here expecting to find paradise." She knew that foreigners often made fun of Israel's "army of girl soldiers" but she regarded this ignorance as being their own bad luck. When I last saw her, she brought a young radioman his evening meal while the deputy commander waited for her to help rearrange some map cases.

This young generation of native-born Israelis inherited certain memories. The soldier-daughter of Colonel Scherman, for instance, was always conscious that her paratroop father was the sole survivor in his family. The rest had perished in Nazi camps. Such knowledge formed a somber background. It colored daily life, for example, in such matters as the absence of aunts and uncles. "In place of blood relatives," she said, "we have close friends of our parents who act as grandpas and cousins and things.

"But we don't like to talk about what happened over there—in Europe. Such terrible things are hard to believe, and I myself don't want to be told that because I'm born a Jew I can arouse these feelings of hatred. We have enough to worry about, building a nation."

In a land where nobody lived beyond the range of Arab shells, the sense of danger was always present. A total boycott prevented any passage across the land frontier. Even nature was hostile. At least half the country needed to be irrigated with water which could be diverted or denied by Arabs. The frontier was open to aggression and over the years it was accepted, or at least assumed, that the United Nations would never stir itself enough to stop the steady Arab shelling of settlements and the sporadic Arab raids and acts of sabotage.

If this was the promised land, many a Jew must have wondered about its name. Israel means "He who struggles with God." Its first premier, David Ben-Gurion, said in a moment of exasperation: "God we can struggle with, but this—?"

The name came from Jacob, whose battle with the Angel of God (Genesis 32:24-28) earned the title Israel. However harsh the 7,993 square miles allotted the Jews, it was more than the fulfillment of a dream. It meant a place on earth where they belonged. "I found," said Ben-Gurion, "the environment I had sought so long. No shopkeepers or speculators, no non-Jewish hirelings or idlers living on the labor of others . . . These were villagers smelling wholesomely of the midden and the ripening ear, and burnt by the sun."

David Ben-Gurion was among those who returned, along with a chunky Ukrainian boy, Levi Eshkol. They stood together this June during the great gamble when aging Israeli armor was pitted against Soviet-built Arab weapons: Ben-Gurion keeping in the background, grimly sure that Israel must take the calculated risk of an overwhelming Arab counterattack, while Eshkol fulfilled his duties as the premier of a government that was no longer in a mood to bargain with an Arab dictator committed to Israel's destruction.

What manner of country, what kind of a people, were they defending? Asked if a third world war might not start here, simply because Israel had no further patience with Nasser, Ben-Gurion growled in reply: "If we wait a moment longer, we shall be like the Jews who walked obediently to their deaths in Nazi extermination centers, and if Israel goes the same way, there is no further hope for humanity."

This tough old man had seen that Israel, to become a nation, required more than independence and territory. It had to have history. The Holocaust, the German destruction of a majority of Europe's Jews, was remembered in the six million trees that reforest the Judean hills. A national hobby was the digging up of past history; the site of Armageddon astride the old routes between Egypt and Mesopotamia where weekend diggers and professional archeologists had bared the remains of 20 cities including that of Solomon; the crusaders' ramparts where Richard the Lion-Hearted fought Saladin at Acre; and the relics of Nazareth.

By the middle of 1967 some 1,500,000 immigrants had settled here since statehood. They came from Asia and Africa as well as Europe but they shared the same awareness of history. They understood the meaning of Herod's tomb in Jerusalem and they regretted the division of the Holy City that denied them access to the Wailing Wall. Out of the first wave of a million settlers, almost half came from Europe and included the scarred survivors of the Nazi camps. Others, often referred to as "Orientals," came from Iran, Morocco, Tunisia, Libya, and Yemen; from Iraq and Turkey and South America.

Internal conflicts arose, inevitably perhaps, because Israel was absorbing Jews of every class. Those from Europe tended to have better educations and greater earning power. The migrations came in waves: sometimes after a sudden lifting of the Iron Curtain; or revolt in Hungary; or expulsion from Egypt after the 1956 Suez campaign. Every Jew upon admission became a citizen with a vote.

Perhaps this rapid growth and efficiency, more than anything else, frightened Arab leaders. Here was a nation governing

21

itself under the same name and in the same territory of 3,000 years ago, employing the same language and following the same religion and certain of its Jewish destiny. These people in a scant 20 years had made the desert bloom. They had returned to what was known as Palestine, where Turks and Arabs for a thousand years permitted neglect and desolation.

"We could wipe out Israel within twelve days," Nasser boasted, but there was hysteria as well as bitterness in his bravado. This land was an intense humiliation to its noisy neighbors. It was regarded as virtually worthless when sold to the early Zionist settlers, and sheer guts and hard work had now turned it into the most valuable real estate in the Middle East.

How this was done is worth recalling.

"Israel has straightened the backs of Jews in every country," declared David Ben-Gurion. "It creates a new image of the Jew—of workers and intellectuals who can fight with heroism."

The old stereotypes were responsible for the prejudices and misjudgments that prevailed until the ovens of Auschwitz forced civilized men to ask where such habits of mind could lead. The Jewish cause became a matter of Western conscience. Until then, a League of Nations mandate over Palestine was held by Britain, whose leaders swung from promising it to the Arabs to offering it to the Jews. By 1947 the so-called Jewish terrorists, often men of scholarship, made it impossible for Britain to govern and so the land was divided between Arabs and Jews by a decision of the UN General Assembly. The Old City of Jerusalem was still denied to the Jews who traditionally bewailed the loss of Zion at the Wailing Wall.

In 1948 the new state had been proclaimed by Ben-Gurion with the words: "In the Land of Israel the Jewish people came into being." Arab reaction was swift and violent. Bombers attacked Tel Aviv on May 15, 1948, and the combined armies of Egypt, Transjordan, Iraq, Lebanon, and Syria moved forward. The Arabs talked of holy war against Jews who had stolen their land, and it was eight months before they were forced to request a ceasefire.

The Jewish colonists had fought off the military might of five sovereign Arab states. But the victory left only bitterness and hatred. The Arabs refused to mark Israel on their maps, and they uttered threats whenever they needed to find some external cause for unity.

"We *have* to find some way to come to terms with the Arab

world," a Jewish publisher and pacifist told me one evening in Jerusalem. He was Uri Avnery, a man widely disliked for his championship of Arab minorities in Israel. "The alternative," he added, "is to have these periodic wars, each worse than the one before."

But Israel, so far, has dealt with each crisis as it arose. The leaders were busy building the new nation and in some ways the external threat helped to create a sense of loyalty and purpose. Soldier-farmers lined the borders, every young man and woman had to serve a period in the armed services, and a militant spirit made it possible for the leaders to demand a great many personal sacrifices. By the practice of austerity and the direction of labor, Israel literally sprang out of the wilderness. This sliver of arid land had been described by English explorers as virtually uninhabitable: it fulfilled the prophecy in Isaiah as a place of dragons "and a court for owls."

To transform it into a land flowing with milk and honey required more than a sense of poetry although there were times when well-wishers seemed inspired by some poetic gift. The WIZO's of Golders Green, for example, were a formidable group of London matrons who regularly erupted on Israel's behalf (WIZO being the acronym for the Women's International Zionist Organization). Donations came from wealthy Jewish families, aid came from the U.S. government ($1.6 billion) and private gifts of money totaled more than $2 billion in the first 16 years, during which Israel tripled its population and raised its gross national product by 10 per cent each year until the standard of living could be compared with that of Western Europe.

Yet Israel was far from being an affluent society. The most casual observer could, if he wished, look beyond the glittering facade of Tel Aviv to become aware of the harsh self-discipline of the people. Struggle had made them lean and leathery. They worked a six-day week and they served as spare-time soldiers and airmen ("Our weekend sailors you need not mention," said a reserve commander. "Not until they get something bigger than kayaks.")

Some of this austerity was in the spirit of the early settlers who founded Histadrut, the labor federation, and the kibbutzim system of communal ownership. This puritan strain is what often repels young North American immigrants, but it suited the grim resolve of the newcomers from Europe. Even today, non-Jewish students are attracted here during their va-

23

cations because of a feeling that individual effort counts; and because Israel breathes a strong sense of purpose in a world which often seems to offer its youth little direction or motive.

The influx of Jews created a great reservoir of intelligence and experience, reflected in the way Israel embarked upon a variety of projects that might have daunted most nations with far better resources of material and money. The key word was self-help. With it, argued the leaders, anything was possible. But this philosophy was a long way from the doctrinaire assertions of such modern dictatorships as communist China, and the Jewish love of argument and dissent made it difficult for any single dogmatist to hold sway.

Israel had run into other difficulties aside from the Arab threat. Unemployment, a word that seemed to have no place in this land echoing to the noise of construction, suddenly became a national scandal. About 100,000 workers, more than 10 per cent of the entire labor force, needed jobs: "For the first time in Israel's history," reported the *Jewish Observer*, ". . . a shock to world Jewry." The journal's editor, Jon Kimche, was dismissed, allegedly for drawing attention abroad to this and other economic setbacks. Kimche replied that it was foolhardy for Israel to stand on its pride to the extent of concealing the facts of an economic downturn. The number of Jewish immigrants fell from the 1949 peak of about 250,-000 to a dribble of 12,000 in 1966; construction was down by 40 per cent and the government put off any new development projects. Gross national product rose by a fraction—1.6 per cent—but was not enough to compensate for the natural growth in population.

The cost of defending Israel against the raids of Arab terrorists became an important factor in the nation's struggle toward prosperity. Young people wanted to enjoy some of the fruits of their labor. Defense chiefs hoarded their relatively small collection of weapons, knowing that each passing year made them more of a liability. There was a demand on one hand for the luxuries that are an everyday part of life in the West; on the other hand, the Chiefs of Staff warned that Israel could not indefinitely improvise with equipment that was being rapidly outclassed by the modern Russian weapons pouring into the surrounding Arab states. Egypt alone had benefited for more than ten years from Russian training and $2 billion worth of Russian jets, tanks, and guns.

Arab raids made life in the border settlements uneasy, and

visitors from abroad frankly voiced their fears that even soldier-farmers could not live indefinitely in such conditions.

Then, early in April 1967, Israeli tractors droned into the "demilitarized zone" on the Syrian frontier to turn the ground for another year's sowing of wheat. At Almagor, a small hilltop settlement in northern Galilee, the drivers could look down on the shallow silver waters of the River Jordan winding to the Sea of Galilee. On the far bank were flat-roofed sandstone Arab huts painted blue to discourage evil spirits. Beyond loomed the snowy peak of Mount Hermon.

The settlement of Almagor is accustomed to hear accusations from the Syrian side at this time of year that the tractors violate the border. Almagor was established by Nahal, the pioneer corps which combines military training with land cultivation so that Israel can defend its frontiers at the same time as it settles the land. The hills are terraced, there are hedges of rosemary, and the air is fragrant with orange blossom.

Syrian guns have shattered the peace of this idyllic scene from time to time, to be answered by Israeli guns. The Arabs have tried here to divert the headwaters of the Jordan, which might otherwise provide a new and precious source of irrigation to the Jewish settlers who everywhere seem obsessed (and rightly so) with the urgent need of more water.

Soon after the Almagor tractors rumbled forth, the scream of MIG-21 jet fighters split the air. In the delta, on the Syrian side, white egrets rose from the backs of black cattle grazing in meadows of lavender thistle and wild mustard. The Russian-built jets dived to the level of the Sea of Galilee and flew low across the border in what appeared to be dummy attacks on the settlement of Almagor. Their pilots pulled up to an altitude of 20,000 feet and the colonists watched the arrowlike wings glint in the sun as the MIG's flipped over for a second plunge.

This intrusion into Israel's air space provoked an instant reaction. The Syrian jets were pounced upon by patrolling Super-Mystères with the Star of David gleaming in blue and white upon their swept wings. The French-built jets were flown by young Israeli pilots who put in more flying time than any other air force men in the world, and they tore into the Syrians with what an American eyewitness described as terrible ferocity.

Six MIG's were claimed totally destroyed (the Syrians claimed four Israeli aircraft) and the wreckage of one was

25

examined and a report sent back to the secret war-room in Tel Aviv, where a number of contingency plans were always ready. The downed MIG bore Polish markings and seemed like a recent and hasty addition to the Syrian store of Russian-made weapons.

Then a month later Syrian terrorists mined a road inside Israel, killing several civilians. A report from intelligence sources in Damascus added to other evidence suggesting the Syrians wanted to provoke Israel so as to force Nasser's Egypt to unleash its power. Guerilla forces supported by Syria revealed a professionalism that was ominous. Once again it seemed as if Arab states were preparing to start another politico-military assault on the morale of the Jews at a time when their homeland seemed most weak and divided.

"If the terrorism continues," warned Israel's premier, "We shall choose the time, the place, and the means to counter the aggressor."

The man who symbolized Arab power was Gamal Abdel Nasser. He seemed to be a victim of his own pressures, obliged to talk tough because he was weak. For a long time he was suspect among other Arab leaders because he refused to declare holy war against Israel. In private he said it was nearly impossible to destroy the Jewish state. To him Egypt's 1958–61 union with Syria was an essential part of the Arab renaissance he sought. Now he seemed to feel he must risk war.

He had achieved much, this son of a postal clerk, since he led a military revolution 15 years ago that destroyed a greedy and odious ruling class in Egypt. He ended the 70-year-old British occupation, won back control of the Suez Canal, launched the imaginative Aswan High Dam, and began the transformation of Egypt into an independent modern state.

At 49 he carried his 6-foot-2 frame and his 220 pounds with the military bearing of a younger man. Only his brooding eyes betrayed an inner obsession. His speeches were reaching new peaks of hysteria. He seemed to be a man running furiously up the down escalator.

Somewhere in his political career Nasser had strayed from the early promise of a young reformist whose personal life was austere and dedicated, whose ambitions were selfless. A flaw in character, a tragic lack of ability to meet the challenges he set himself, made him depend upon doubtful allies and look to strange and vicious men for inspiration. He wanted to unite the Arabs in a single crescent curving from the Atlantic to the borders of Turkey. He did not regard Israel as the main enemy. He feared and hated the Great Powers far more, especially the United States and Britain. Others, notably the German Nazis he hired, inflamed anti-Jewish sentiments among the Moslems into a campaign of violent hate.

Nasser was born on January 15, 1918, in a suburb of Alexandria. (Moshe Dayan was then a three-year-old kibbutz boy living less than 300 miles away.) He attended Egypt's military academy and as the founder of the Committee of Free Officers to Overthrow the Government, he destroyed the corrupt and self-indulgent leaders around King Farouk whom he sent into exile. Two years later, in 1954, Nasser took full power. From that time on, he followed the classic path of all dictators. His political intelligence was distorted by a conspiratorial nature. He was less and less able to accept criticism and he soon believed his own propagandists. Twice he was led into war by his own emotionalism and a gambler's passion for shortcuts to success.

Some change took place in Nasser's outlook however in 1960 when the union with Syria (which led to the formation of the United Arab Republic, a name Egypt still retains without much justification) ran into trouble. Nasser himself had escaped blame for the Suez debacle by claiming that Anglo-French air power was responsible for his defeat at the hands of the Israeli armies. But he believed that Syria's withdrawal from the union was the work of Western agents.

Syria pulled out in 1961, and Iraq refused to take its place in the federation. This aroused Nasser to greater revolutionary efforts; and instead of analyzing the egotism of the Syrians, and thus discovering the root cause of his failures in that direction, Nasser proclaimed his People's Charter for the Arabs and codified his socialist ideology.

Outside of Egypt, the Arabs watched him with an increasingly rheumy eye. His armies in Yemen, for a short time, won back for him a certain amount of respect; his troops fought in support of a republican regime which had overthrown a widely despised ruling family; but then the Egyptian forces bogged down in what promised to be an interminable conflict.

When Nasser imperiously summoned the Arab heads of state to Cairo in January 1965 it was already evident that events were running against him. The Arab world suffered from internal squabbles, economic decline, and differing concepts of what was meant by Arab nationalism.

Then came an alleged attack by Israeli forces on the Jordan village of Samoue in November 1966. King Hussein was condemned by Egypt and Syria for failing to defend the village. He taunted Egypt in return, claiming Nasser sheltered behind the United Nations Emergency Force.

Egypt signed a joint defense agreement with Syria, whose government was calling for a more militant policy toward Israel. The demands on Nasser were awkward. He could not ignore an ally's requests for more aid unless he wished to abdicate from his position as self-proclaimed leader of the Arab world. Already he faced a strong rival in King Faisal of Saudi Arabia who had launched an "Islamic Alliance." By this time it was impossible for Nasser to climb down from any position; and the only direction in which he could move was up, even if it meant an ascent to disaster.

His first move of any consequence involved the United Nations Emergency Force (UNEF), which had been stationed on the Egyptian side of the Egyptian-Israeli border as a precaution against further hostilities after the 1956 conflict. UNEF in many ways suited Nasser, whose armies were not yet ready for another trial of strength with Israel, although they were superbly equipped and far superior in numbers. But Nasser had talked so much about "the liberation struggle" that other Arab states jeered at the UN "pane of glass" which saved Egypt from the need to act upon its own advice to others. The great crusader was asked to match deeds with words. It was not enough for Nasser to move his troops around the Israeli border, and claim he was fulfilling his defense agreement with Syria in this fashion. The UN still sealed the border, and the question was asked if Nasser really had any intention of backing Syrian demands that Israel behave herself (demands which, if obeyed, seemed only to foreshadow Israel's emasculation and eventual end).

Then on the evening of Wednesday, May 17, 1967, a cable arrived in New York from the UNEF commander, Major-General Indar Jit Rikhye of India. The cable was addressed to the UN Secretary-General, U Thant, who was dressing to go out for dinner. It said the Egyptians had asked that all UN troops withdraw from the 117-mile Israeli-Egyptian frontier and move to the relative security of the Gaza Strip. The explanation for this surprising request, offered by Egyptian Chief of Staff Mohammed Fawzi, was that he did not wish UN troops to get hurt in any clash between his forces and those of Israel.

U Thant's reaction later caused worldwide argument and much bitter criticism. He informed the Egyptian president that a temporary pullback was not possible but, on the other hand, Egypt had a right to ask for the complete withdrawal of UN forces. The matter was not referred to the UN Security Council, nor to the General Assembly. Meanwhile Nasser could hardly fail to request a complete withdrawal. U Thant promptly gave the order to evacuate.

In the confused aftermath, diplomats quarreled over whether or not this order pushed Nasser toward war. It robbed Egypt of any further excuse not to stand eyeball to eyeball with Israel, as the other Arab states had been demanding. "If war breaks out," commented the London *Spectator,* "historians may well come to look back on it as U Thant's war." It called his action precipitate, high-handed, and grossly irresponsible. Officials in Washington were quoted as calling it "monumentally stupid." But there were others who defended U Thant and contended that no legal grounds existed for keeping UNEF on Egyptian soil since the forces were there only at Egypt's request.

The further excuse, that Egypt had delivered an ultimatum and therefore U Thant could not risk the safety of UNEF troops, could only increase Israel's apprehension. For whatever the sophisticated arguments might be, conducted in the remote sanctuary of the UN, Israel was now confronted with the problem of trying to divine Arab intentions.

U Thant claimed he acted to save the UNEF troops.* Did

---

* A version of events given by Ralph Bunche, a veteran Mideast peace-maker and now UN Under Secretary, was this:

"On the night of May 16 the [Egyptian] demand was received by UNEF for removal of 'all UN troops installed at Observation Posts along our borders.' This unquestionably included Sharm el Sheikh . . . A movement of [Egyptian] troops up to the line in Sinai quickly followed. The [Egyptian] Chief of Staff then demanded at midday on May 17 local time that all UNEF detachments should be withdrawn from Sinai, *specifically including Sharm el Sheikh.* In fact his troops arrived to take over the UN camp and positions at Sharm el Sheikh and Ras Nasrani at 12:10 hours GMT on May 18, demanding a response from UN troops there within fifteen minutes. They did not get it, and the UNEF troops remained there for six more days, although they were unable to function. The official request for the withdrawal of UNEF was received by the UN Secretary-General at 12 noon New York time on May 18, i.e. some four hours after the actual arrival of [Egyptian] troops at Sharm el Sheikh.

29

he, then, know more than he was admitting about Arab plans for aggression? The question might seem ridiculous in the calm atmosphere of New York but it was charged with emotion for the people of Israel.

"There was the long history of Arab attacks, to begin with," said a Jewish scientist. "But also in every mind was the recollection of what happened in Europe, and the haunting fear that perhaps we might have done something to save the victims of Nazi extermination. None of us wanted war—good God! Most of us had lived through three wars. Yet the evacuation of the UNEF forces seemed like a warning we couldn't ignore. If we did, we could only blame ourselves for what happened after."

In Tel Aviv there was a sudden sense of abnormal tension. Veterans of other trouble spots, in other times, recognized the symptoms. It was the week of Independence Day celebrations. The traditional military parade through Jerusalem was boycotted by foreign ambassadors of the major powers, a token of the disapproval abroad of suggestions that Israel might attack the Syrian capital of Damascus, reputedly the oldest continuously inhabited city in the world, and now agitated by Arab demands to "destroy the Jews."

Until this time, it was still possible to regard these events as another typical Mideast crisis. Nasser seemed to have scored a diplomatic coup by moving into Sinai and Gaza, dismissing UN forces, and putting himself in a position to deter Israel from any action against Syria.

But then he announced on May 22 that "under no circumstances will we allow the Israeli flag to pass through the Aqaba Gulf." The Voice of the Arabs broadcast on Radio Cairo: "We pity you Jews. By God, we pity you. This is our revenge for Suez and the 1956 aggression."

The reason for the UN Secretary-General's position that UNEF could not accept an order to withdraw from one part of the line and remain on another part was that to do this would in fact make UNEF a party to the resumption of war by opening the door to a direct military confrontation between Israel and Egypt. The latter, once it decided to move its troops to any part of the line, ended UNEF's usefulness. The line UNEF covered was 295 miles with a total force of 3,400 (1,800 on the line) with personal arms for defense only. At Sharm el Sheikh 32 men were stationed."

CHAPTER FOUR

WHEN IS A WAR NOT A WAR? asked the London *Observer* on May 28, echoing a question that disturbed the Israeli cabinet, now balanced between a decision to hit the menacing Arab armies or give diplomacy a last chance. Nasser's blockade of the Gulf of Aqaba seemed clearly to have overstepped all limits, and yet there was a deep Israeli concern for world opinion.

Attention was focused upon the Strait of Tiran and the barrier of islands and reefs that forces all shipping bound for the Gulf of Aqaba to enter a narrow channel commanded by Egyptian guns on the clifftop stronghold of Sharm el Sheikh. Until the Suez campaign of 1956 when Israeli forces captured the point, Egypt had refused passage to any Israeli vessel seeking to navigate the 115-mile gulf to the new port of Elath. Then for a time it seemed safe to assume that the UN would guarantee freedom of passage, since the stronghold had been abandoned by Israeli forces on the understanding that a UN garrison would hold it.

The dismissal of UN forces, however, cleared the way for Nasser's 1967 declaration of a blockade. By doing this, he struck at Israel's communications with Africa and Asia. He rendered the port of Elath useless. And Elath handled almost 90 per cent of Israel's vital oil supplies arriving from Iranian ports on the Persian Gulf, as well as a growing Israeli trade with East Africa, India, and the East.

Elath was Israel's dramatic reply to Nasser's long-standing denial of the Suez Canal to her ships. Ten years ago the port simply did not exist. It was the place where the people of Exodus regrouped after their miraculous passage through the Red Sea and out of Egypt.

Elath sat at the head of the Gulf of Aqaba, compressed between Egypt on the west and Jordan to the east. It provided a dangerously tiny slit through which Israeli traders could make contact with the developing countries of Afro-Asia— "the third world" of immense potential which Israel's diplomats and economists were hoping would provide markets and work for the young state.

An outsider needs to be reminded that Egypt's policy on waterways was vitally important to Israel. General Moshe Dayan had written, after the 1956 Suez campaign: "One of the basic issues in the conflict between Israel and Egypt was the freedom of Israeli shipping through the Red Sea." Vessels had to pass through the Suez Canal if they wished to reach the Red Sea from the Israeli port of Haifa; and ships leaving Elath in the southernmost tip of Israel had to cross the Strait of Tiran. It had been Egyptian policy to bar these waterways to Israeli shipping and thus to deny Israel direct naval communication with East Africa and Asia. "Israel," wrote General Dayan, "is not rich in natural resources, and among the few minerals she does possess, potash and phosphates take first place and are exported primarily to countries of the Far East. Blocking naval routes to this region was . . . a grave blow." In September 1955 the Gulf of Aqaba had been declared closed to Israel ships and planes because Egypt considered a state of war to exist. Furthermore, the Israeli national airline El Al had been warned to stop flights to South Africa, so that the scope of the Egyptian blockade of Suez and Tiran had now been seriously widened. On December 5, 1955, General Dayan had written David Ben-Gurion an official letter proposing "the capture of the Strait of Tiran" on the grounds that Egypt's actions would lead to the loss of Israel's naval and aerial freedom, whereby "Elath becomes for us a coastal strip along a closed lake, exit from which will be conditional on Egyptian agreement."

In every developing Afro-Asian country the Israelis in the 1960's were seeking business and influence, and Elath was a vital part of long-range plans for making Israel share in the future growth and prosperity of the so-called backward countries, with their reserves of natural and unexploited wealth. In the former wards and colonies of the West, the ambassadors of Israel could point to the accomplishments of the past twenty years in their own land, and urge newly independent governments to follow suit.

Israel's activities were more than a nuisance to the Communist powers, seeking to strengthen and broaden their position in the Afro-Asian world. The Peking government was especially blunt in denouncing Israel as an imperialist pawn. China's Communists were forever urging the Arab states to destroy Israel, in theory because she represented a deviation in socialist ideology, and in truth because Israel's socialists had already influenced some of the Southeast Asian countries China sought to dominate.

It must have seemed a brilliant move to Nasser when he closed the Elath door in 1967 after Israel had opened it in 1956 by capturing Sharm el Sheikh which it later relinquished. In a stroke he stopped the shipment of Israeli goods to Ethiopia, Burma, Malaya, Vietnam, Japan, and Australia, at a time when his enemy's economy could scarcely take the strain. He could strangle the infant tire industry which imported rubber from Singapore and reexported through Elath to Iran. He could make nonsense of all the effort that had gone into building a city in this inhospitable place where rainfall and underground desert water together only supplied three-quarters of local water requirements.

The threat to Elath set in motion the secret machinery of Israel's plans for a preventive war. The words "preventive" and "preemptive" were academic in the circumstances, since it was clear by now that the Arab supporters of President Nasser claimed for themselves the right to take whatever initiative they wished in their campaign to eliminate the Jews from what they insisted was Arab soil. But Israel's defense chiefs continued to heed the advice of diplomats and politicians that it would be dangerous to be condemned as the first to strike a military blow.

There were other considerations. Premier Levi Eshkol was far from sure that Israel could endure a war lasting more than a week. The arithmetic of power was all too simple. His forces, armed with a mixture of American, British, and French weapons, were limited in range and endurance by very ordinary problems of logistics and performance. "I know our men are better trained," he said impatiently to one of his close political friends. "I also know they're fighting with their backs to the sea. But a catapult against a rocket is still a catapult."

He knew that Soviet Russian technical advisors were serving with Syrian forward units. He knew Russia had committed her reputation in backing the Arabs. He knew that Egyptian prisoners, kidnapped by Israeli desert patrols, had disclosed the existence of missiles capable of knocking out Israel's main defenses. He knew the Israeli air force, constantly filming the Arab positions from high altitude, had confirmed the positions of high-performance Russian jets and missiles and the assembly of front-line Egyptian forces just across the Suez Canal in the Sinai Peninsula.

An operational order, dated May 21, 1967, instructed the Eastern Air Region of the United Arab Republic on the priority of bombing targets in Israel. It was signed by Jelal Ibrahim Ziz, the Egyptian Eastern Air Command chief-of-staff, and it stressed the importance of striking the first blow.

Despite a feeling that the wrong word might bring Arab arms toppling down upon Israel, Premier Eshkol issued a warning in the Knesset, the Israeli Parliament, that any interference with the freedom of shipping would be taken as an act of aggression "and a gross violation of international law."

The legal position was not clear, however. The Tiran channel passed through Egyptian territorial waters. On the other hand, no ship could approach a port to the north of the narrow gulf without passing through the territorial waters of Israel, Jordan, and Saudi Arabia as well as Egypt. In theory any of these states could prevent vessels reaching any other of the littoral states, and special rules applied to such a waterway. The generally accepted rule was that whoever controlled the passage should allow "free and innocent passage." This rule was explicitly upheld by the United States in a 1957 aide-memoire to Israel, but it was possible to argue about the term "innocent passage."

The Geneva Conference of 1958, Article 16(4) of the Convention on the High Seas in the Contiguous Zone, declared there should be "no suspension of the innocent passage of foreign ships through straits used for international navigation between one part of the high seas and . . . the territorial sea of a foreign State."

The right of innocent passage through Egyptian waters had been admitted by an Egyptian representative to the Security Council long ago, but he added: "The passage of contraband of war through the national and territorial waters of Egypt to Israel is certainly not a case of innocent passage. It violates the most explicit provisions of Egyptian law (listing contraband goods including food) and strengthens Israel's war effort."

Egypt insisted that she was at war with Israel and had been since 1948, and an Egyptian diplomat reinforced the argument in a letter to the *Guardian* in London on May 23, 1967. He said the Egyptian government considered Article 16(4) applicable only in times of peace and "not in the area where there is a state of war between the Arab States and Israel."

Thus the Arab states denied freedom of navigation to ships bound for Elath on grounds that a state of war allegedly divided Egypt and Israel, with consequent belligerency rights.

This was the basis on which Nasser was banning Israel's ships from the Suez Canal. His application of the same ban to the Gulf of Aqaba, and Cairo's boast that the waters had been mined, faced the Israeli government with a new crisis it could not shirk.

"I think we might have dodged the issue," said Israel's foreign minister, Abba Eban, in a later conversation, "if we were not in a peculiar and unique position of being a nation composed of people who had some knowledge of where compromise can lead."

International lawyers were ready enough to argue the question of belligerency rights, said to be excluded by an armistice agreement between Egypt and Israel of 1949. Such legalistic disputes were only too familiar to Israel's leaders, who must have listened with sinking spirits to the laconic proceedings at the Security Council. There almost half the members lined up obediently behind the Soviet Union, whose representative blandly declared that no justification existed in this third week of May 1967 for the calling of an emergency session.

"Know what you fight for and love what you know," Oliver Cromwell had instructed his men. The quotation was familiar to Jewish soldiers who had served with Orde Wingate,* that strangely inspired Englishman who organized special night squads among the settlers to protect installations against Arab saboteurs. The words echoed again in the hearts of Israel's modern army commanders as they heard the diplomats once again confuse what had seemed to be a clearcut issue. To them Nasser's blockade might have some legality but it was demonstrably one more slice of the salami. It had the same validity as the Russian delivery of missiles to Cuba in 1962, the kind of

---

* Orde Wingate, a commando and jungle warfare expert, helped to lay the foundations of the modern Israeli forces, which inherited from him a belief in the advantages of surprise and imaginative tactics.

action which demanded a response from the nation thus challenged. "You either stood firm at this point," said Menahem Begin, "or you ceased to exist."

When I talked with Begin on the last day of that critical month of May, the showdown with Arab forces only a few days away, he had been asked to join a coalition government. His appointment as Minister Without Portfolio, together with the cooption of Major-General Moshe Dayan as Minister for Defense, should have been a sufficient warning to the encircling Arabs and their Russian supporters that somewhere in the hearts of all Israeli citizens a decision had been taken.

There was no self-deception involved. The leaders of Israel, now including men who differed on many political issues in peacetime, were resigned to one fact: nobody was going to help them if it came to a trial of strength. The Western powers betrayed an overwhelming anxiety to avert a full-scale conflict and urged Israel to postpone any military reaction to the blocking of the Gulf of Aqaba. Those Arab propaganda agencies serving President Nasser flooded newspaper offices with "facts" to show that Israel scarcely used the Gulf and hardly needed the port of Elath anyway. France, which had once seemed a friend to Israel, made an expedient adjustment in policy to reassure her more rewarding Arab partners that she felt no sympathy for the Jewish case.

A new U.S. ambassador to Cairo, Richard Nolte, celebrated his appointment by delivering a disagreeable message to President Nasser: the use of force could not be excluded in restoring Israel's access to the Gulf of Aqaba.

This sounded to Israel like a gesture from Washington, designed as much to prevent or at least discourage some precipitate action by the Israeli armies as it was to impress Nasser. The likelihood was that Nasser would pay small attention to such a muted warning, since he had the Russians clearly on his side both in the UN and in their physical support.

Britain supported a call for open passage through the Strait of Tiran, but this too sounded more like a pious hope than a call to action. It was obvious that Britain would wish to avoid a repetition of the 1956 Suez affair when she lost Afro-Asian friends and suffered a deep domestic wound.

Israel, aware of widespread sympathy but resigned to the probability that she would have to fight her own way out of the Arab ring, either through diplomacy or more likely by a trial of strength, put into motion a carefully considered plan.

This was designed to bring the nation into a condition of total war readiness without imperiling any diplomatic moves that might yet lift the Arab threat.

The series of cryptic radio announcements transformed civilians into soldiers. In the bare drift sands of the Negev Desert, the biblical Wilderness of Zin, the colonels of the armored units had their orders. Under their command were tanks and armored vehicles that could move with great speed behind the enemy, and split into smaller independent forces, always self-sustaining. By Friday, May 26, 1967, these forces were ready to roll.

Part II: Struggle

CHAPTER FIVE

If you say in your heart "These nations
are more than I and how can I dispossess them?"
you shall not fear them but remember what the
Lord thy God did unto Pharaoh and unto all Egypt.
—Deuteronomy 7:17–18

Monday, June 5

*Israel is roughly the size of New Jersey. It is long and thin—
260 miles from north to south, and seventy miles at its widest,
tapering to the six-mile strip of coastline on the Gulf of Aqaba
where another attempted Egyptian blockade, a repetition of
the first twelve years before, triggered the war.*

*The capital, Jerusalem, is on the same latitude as Los
Angeles. To visit there is to make an "aliyah" or going-up, a
kind of spiritual ascent. The Old City had been more or less
denied the Jews for 896 years until the forces of Jordan were
smashed in the lightning attack of June 1967. Leading the hit
parade at the time was a new song: "Jerusalem of gold, of
copper, and of light . . ."*

*Tel Aviv is the coastal city of white concrete cubes and
curving beaches, a place of commerce and pleasure.*

*The jets and tanks and troops that sprang out of this com-
pact country were concealed within four distinct regions. To
understand the events of June 5 to June 12, 1967, it is useful
to keep these regions in mind.*

The coastal plain *lies between the sea and the hills, flanking
the Mediterranean from Rosh ha-Nikra on the Lebanese
frontier to the Gaza Strip where some of the worst fighting
took place. This was the coastal route of ancient imperial
armies and trading caravans between the Nile Valley and
Mesopotamia. Underground springs keep the light sandy soil
fertile.*

The Negev *is known in the Bible as the Wilderness of Zin,
and here the armored units learned to move with speed and*

imagination. It accounts for 55 per cent of Israel's land area, but it supports the smallest number of people. This sparse plain is being opened up for settlement. Enormous pipelines have started its irrigation. South of the atomic research center near Beersheba it becomes bleaker as it narrows down to the head of the Gulf of Aqaba between the Sinai and Jordan borders.

The Jordan Valley *opens the longest rift in the earth's surface, a giant crack that crosses the Red Sea and stabs deep into Africa's heart. The Jordan River has been a cause of enmity between Arabs and Jews who badly needed to share its waters. In fact the river is startlingly small, a mere stream, flowing out of Mount Hermon, down the Huleh Valley, and through the Sea of Galilee. It ends at the Dead Sea. The trough of the Jordan Valley continues along the Israel border to the Gulf of Aqaba.*

The Hill Country *forms a backbone of porous limestone. Most of it consists of worn hills and wadis. The Galilee highlands, in the north, are separated from the Mountains of Samaria and Judea by a valley that runs southeast across the land. These hills produce rain during the short winter.*

The rain fell, to everyone's surprise, during the mini-war. The big raindrops that splattered across flat rooftops during the night in Tel Aviv were taken as an omen. People remembered that snow had fallen during the previous winter around Jerusalem, which is also unusual. The harvest was abnormally good in this year of signs and portents. And in the moment of triumph a great many Israelis turned to their Bibles for other words of prophecy, for the sense of Jewish destiny is a strong one. The landscape encourages this awareness of a biblical past. The cypresses are like dark green candles against the blue sky. The palms are like reeds that bend in the wind. There is stark simplicity in the combination of sand, sea and sky. On such a battlefield, the words of a commander must fall inevitably into the sonorous rhythm of a prophet's language: "The battle is over but there is no end yet to our struggle," said General Dayan. "Those who rose up against us have been vanquished but they have yet to make peace. Return your swords to your scabbards but keep them ready, for the time has not yet come when you may beat them into plowshares."

Jets exploded out of Israel like bolts of lightning preceding the dawn. They arrived with the sun over the Egyptian airbases at Alexandria and Gamil, at Abu Sueir, Deversoir, and

Fayid, at Luxor and Almaza and Cairo West. Their pilots were anonymous youths, from the farming kibbutzim for the most part, like their commander.

He alone was named. Air Brigadier Mordecai Hod protected the fliers from Arab guerillas by issuing a blanket order to conceal their identities. It was part of his passion for secrecy— an overriding sense of the importance of denying the enemy any premature disclosure of the facts about the terrible swift sword with which Israel cut down her enemies, and virtually guaranteed within the first three hours of this vengeful week the final victory.

In precise and thunderous arcs, out over the Mediterranean and low beneath the radar, his lovely Mirage–3's and Super-Mystères flew toward the slumbering targets. They burst out of Israeli bases, some of which many citizens had never dreamed existed, and in the first massive strike they clung together until they were lost in sea mist and then they split: one group screaming across the desert to approach Cairo from the southwest, another turning directly inland from the north. They flew at 500 feet and slammed new and secret 12-foot directional bombs into some 200 front-line Egyptian fighter jets, mostly MIG–21's, dozing in their revetments.

More Israeli jets hammered the enemy's air bases in the Sinai, in Jordan, Syria, and Iraq. Each strike was followed by another. Some pilots flew eight missions before the day was ended. Some were bronzed teenagers who had been driving tractors the week before, and God willing would drive them again a week from now: boys of eighteen who flew in tight-lipped silence, observing radio silence, each riding a massive jet engine that packed more power than an entire World War II squadron. Some were middle-aged men with memories of footslogging with General Anders' Polish troops. And a few were professional airline captains snatched from the crew cabins of El Al's Boeing–707's. They made up the most effective fighting machine, weight for weight, in the world.

They raked the Arab bases with rockets and 30–mm cannon fire when their bombs were gone. They swept onto their targets at top speed, some cracking sound barriers above the tawny hills of Lower Egypt and the scrublands fringing the Western Desert, others skimming the flat coastline of the Nile Delta. But when they descended upon the Russian jets obligingly lined up like droopy-winged moths, they dropped brake flaps and undercarriages to cut their speed, and slowly and precisely

40

they destroyed the Arab warplanes which were Israel's greatest concern. By the time UN delegates in New York were thinking of collective security, by the time the machinery was being cranked into action for calling a session of the Security Council, the 25 most vital air bases in the Arab world had been tidily wrecked.

"Almost every Israeli plane collected bulletholes from small-arms fire," said General Dayan, explaining the surgical skill with which the pilots cut out the lethal bases. Aerial photos later revealed Arab planes squashed in the sand with scarcely a bomb scar in the neighboring landscape. Bombs were not wasted on the dummy MIGs which had been staked out as decoys. This selectivity aroused the curiosity of Western air attachés who were not told of a new Israeli device for homing bombs onto live targets only.

When the Security Council finally assembled at 10:30 A.M. in New York, it was already 4:30 P.M. in Israel and the first tallies were showing 280 Egyptian aircraft destroyed on the ground and another 20 in the air; 52 destroyed in Syria, 20 in Jordan, and 7 in Iraq. That first savage strike had already decided the issue in the air, and the way was clear for Israeli armor to race forward and capture as much territory as possible before the UN collected its wits and agreed upon a ceasefire call.

The aerial victory did not guarantee an easy advance for the columns of armor, which relied upon surprise and mobility to throw the Egyptians off balance. It did mean lifting a black cloud of anxiety for desert commanders who wanted to fight with their eyes facing front, and not turned skyward.

"We had absolute confidence in the air force," said Brigadier-General Israel Tal, commanding the armored corps, who had himself personally led one of the three major armored assaults. "We were using old tanks, tanks dating from the Second World War. The enemy, both in Egypt and Syria, had the most modern tanks—some were acquired even before they were introduced into Soviet divisions. The Egyptians had moved fighting units from Yemen and they brought seven divisions into Sinai against our three divisions. We needed complete mastery in the air."

The mobilization of Egyptian troops in the Sinai Peninsula was given as the reason for Israel's actions; that and "movements toward us," and the appearance on Israeli radar screens of Egyptian MIG's "in considerable numbers" heading for

Tel Aviv. There was an air-raid alarm at 7:55 A.M. and five minutes later Brigadier-General Yeshayahu Gavish, commanding the southern front, received the order to advance. "The enemy began it," said this balding soldier later, thumbs hooked into the belt of his denims—challenging his inquisitor to doubt the truth of it, his hard blue eyes steady and surrounded by laughter crinkles.

Did the Egyptians cross the frontier? If so, where? The questions were pressed upon Foreign Minister Abba Eban. "In any case," he said blandly, "their shells did."

Whatever the facts, there was not a single foreign correspondent to be found in Israel during the preceding week who did not believe this country was obliged to go to war. "My only fear," said James Cameron, covering his tenth war for the BBC and London papers, "is that Israel may underestimate the enemy." Like others, he wondered about the German-model rockets and the Russian missiles, and speculated about Communist intentions as Russian warships moved into the Mediterranean. "Civilization as we know it started here," said Ben Oyserman, a CBS cameraman. "Perhaps this is where it's going to end." The end was already near for Oyserman, who was to be killed next day, but his forebodings, like those of others, were to prove unfounded. And like the others, he faced the possibility of catastrophe with jaunty calm.

For days the reservists had moved to their posts, wearing a mixture of army levis and beach shirts, struggling into bush jackets and toting knapsacks. Eight days earlier, the younger ones had received wives and sweethearts at their army posts which were, in theory, secretly located. In a country so small, it required little skill to trace the men and no time at all to catch a bus to the front.

In the Negev Desert waited the tanks, each with one member from Israel's 51,200-man regular army. During the preceding nights, the tank crews had been made up by the reservists: a waiter from a Tel Aviv restaurant perhaps, and a Haifa fisherman with his cousin from the local dairy. Three reservists were required to make up each tank's crew.

"In the first few tanks that broke through to join us," Brigadier-General Abraham Yoffe was to say later, "I saw my brother's boy, who is a tank commander, and I can tell you it was a very moving moment when I saw and recognized him there."

42

He was describing the initial thrust of his own armored mobile division. To hear these generals later—with their evocative names like Israel and Abraham and Ariel—was like eavesdropping on a family discussion. It was one reason for their swift triumph. They knew, with the intimacy of the fireside, each other's capacities and limits. "The trouble with our armies," Yoffe himself complained, "is that the corporal says one thing and the captain says another, and they all want to take the initiative. Once early in the battle I heard somebody ask permission to take another route, and when I asked him why, he said, 'Well, there's a bunch of Arab tanks over there,' and I told him to stick his nose into his own business. They kept trying to find their own individual enemy and trying to engage him and destroy him, and then when we hit the Canal one of my commanders asked permission to wash his feet in it, and it was the first I knew that we'd arrived, and I told him No and his feet are still not washed."

These laconic stories were to be told after the battles. The desert war began in disciplined order. A superb organization had been created for fielding a fighting force of 234,700 men, almost five times the size of the standing army and about half the total male population of military age, within 48 hours. Buses took reservists to their units, but many hitchhiked, and some drove up in their own laundry trucks and milk wagons.

"I must tell you, my troops looked a real mob," said Brigadier-General Ariel Sharon, a paratroop commander who took a division to force a way through an Egyptian brigade blocking the Mitla Pass. "I mean, they're wonderful soldiers, but they were not—well, properly dressed, and they had all kinds of civilian vehicles, what we call '*thuva* lorries,' or milk trucks, and I wondered what the Egyptian prisoners of war would think when they saw these soldiers, my men, and their vehicles . . ."

Because they knew each other by their first names, commanders and men, there was little need for talk. Instead of the babel of voices that chokes the radio transmitters of modern Western armies in times of stress, Israel gathered her strength by stealth. There was a terse announcement 30 minutes after the first air-raid siren over Radio Kol Israel: "Heavy fighting has begun against Egyptian armor and aerial forces." The theme song from *The Bridge on the River Kwai* was mixed in with Jewish folksongs and the Battle Hymn of the Israeli Armored Corps, and every hour on the hour came more news, cold and factual. The war had started with only the older reservists still to be mobilized, and from time to time new code names were heard: Alternating Current, Good Friends, Open Window . . .

"It was such a blessed relief," said Rinna Samuel, a former New York schoolteacher who worked with her husband at the Weizmann Institute. "The tensions of the last hours of peace had been so great. We were so sure we were going to be attacked and it didn't seem worth doing anything. You know, people went to work and the kids went to school but these were routine things and all the time we'd been waiting for the balloon to go up. There'd been a full blackout on Sunday night and everyone sat around and speculated, and wondered if the government might just keep this up for weeks, so we'd be sitting in our thousands in blacked-out rooms in a state of psychological siege. And of course by then the only civilians were women and children and older men, and a lot of *those* were on duty as air-raid wardens. And so that Monday morning was a kind of blessing."

Air Brigadier Hod felt the same relief for different reasons. He was the 41-year-old son of an Israeli farmer and he understood very well the problems of the foot soldier. He had served in World War II as a British infantry officer. His air force was fighting fit but it numbered less than 350 warplanes and most of these came from France whose swing toward pro-Arab policies might affect supplies. His jets were constantly ready for battle and this meant a steady draining of strength, for the crews were flying around the clock and the needle-nosed planes demanded the most devoted care. Each day of waiting had caused a tiny but irreversible loss in efficiency. Modern aircraft age quickly. Parts wear out and cannot be easily repaired by improvisation. Long before the war began, Brigadier Hod faced the question of how much longer he could promise the land forces the air cover they needed.

"We had to stretch an air umbrella that was built for light rain, not a torrential thunderstorm," said one of his staff officers, a physicist by trade. First, in the prewar days when Nasser's Arabs were calling for a holy war, and we couldn't hit back, the jets were needed to fight off intruders and to watch the surrounding states for any signs of a synchronized attack. Second, we had to keep a sufficient number of fighters in the air at all times against the possibility of a surprise air offensive—and the combined air forces of our enemies totaled

44

more than 800 high-performance jets, mostly Russian. Third, if war came, we had to have a striking force to knock out as many Arab bases as possible.

"And finally, we owed it to our soldiers to give them absolute confidence. We'd worked out the closest coordination, for instance, between tanks and jets."

Pilots had debated the situation after Egypt closed the Gulf of Aqaba. "We worried about fuel reserves," said one. "We worried about shipment of the things that feed a jet. We knew if the call to strike came, we'd smash our enemies. But how long could we endure the prelude to war?"

So there had always been a time limit on the "peace" that preceded the moment when General Dayan declared: "Soldiers, on this day our hopes and security are with you."

This time limit was coldly measured by Israel's computers. Like the reservists on whom everything depended, these computers did double-duty. In their civilian capacity they served the scientists in Tel Aviv and Beersheba, but they also analyzed the state of military preparedness. Some weeks earlier, in one of the periodic reports submitted to the defense chiefs by the highly secret Committee for Strategic Studies, the conclusion had been drawn that Israel was like an aging lion whose fangs could not be replaced and whose teeth must soon drop out. The nation's weaponry was being slowly outclassed by the equipment bestowed upon the surrounding Arab states; and even if Israel could afford to buy guns and warplanes and tanks to match, it was doubtful if she could obtain them in sufficient quantity. Her own arms industry was insignificant against this growth of Communist-supplied Arab power. And finally, Israel's economy could not withstand an arms race.

Nasser only needed, in fact, to wait. It was the one thing he failed to do, said Foreign Minister Abba Eban in a speech to the Security Council after the war began. "Nasser brought five infantry divisions and two armored divisions up to our very gates: 80,000 men and 900 tanks were poised to move. A special striking force comprising an armored division with at least 200 tanks was concentrated against Elath at the Negev's southern tip. Here was a clear design to cut the southern Negev off from the main body of our State. For Egypt had openly proclaimed that Elath did not form part of Israel and had predicted that Israel itself would soon expire . . . For 16 years Israel had been illicitly denied passage in the Suez Canal and now the creative enterprise of ten patient years which had opened an international route across the Strait of Tiran and the Gulf of Aqaba had been suddenly and arbitrarily choked. Israel was and is breathing with only a single lung."

Egypt had made it possible for Israel to escape the calendar's peacetime logic. There was, however, another time factor, and again the computers had worked out the awesome equation. Once hostilities began, Israel's armor must knock out the enemy within ten days, and preferably in five.

"Once the Arab air fields were rendered unserviceable," reported the Chief of General Staff, Major-General Yitzhak Rabin, "the burden fell upon our desert units."

The thrust of armor had been carefully plotted by Rabin. His commanders were briefed so completely upon contingency plans, anticipating a variety of emergencies, that once ordered to move, they knew exactly what was required. Rabin had been a commando in the Haganah at the age of 18 and his entire adult life was that of a professional soldier. Born in Jerusalem 45 years earlier, he had worked under British direction as a World War II saboteur. He had fought against the British when they opposed Jewish immigration to Palestine. He was a farmer by inclination and he embodied those contradictory features that characterize the Israeli: a tough no-nonsense approach to the arts of war, and the kind of gentleness under fire that was to impress itself upon foreign observers during the blitzkrieg-type campaign he now launched.

"The main arena of action was the Sinai Peninsula," said General Gavish of Southern Command. "There were three principal axes. First the coastal axis from Rafah to the Canal. Then the axis from Ketziot to Abu Aweigila. Finally the axis Kuntilla-A'Temed-E'Nahl-Port Fuad-Suez."

These were the East-West routes which were few, rough, and divided by bony ridges of rock and shifting seas of sand. Movement along them was at any time difficult. Now the Israeli forces were opposed by the best of Egyptian armor.

Rabin and his brilliant deputy, General Haim Barlev, had defined their broad objectives as the breaking of this mass of Arab armor between the Negev and Suez, to be followed by a sprint south to grab Sharm el Sheikh and the heights that controlled the Strait of Tiran. (The two men who were forging victory were later content to see the credit go to General Dayan. Neither Rabin, a graduate of a British Staff College in addition to being a former anti-British guerilla, nor Barlev, a Columbia University graduate born in Yugoslavia, had much time for the theatrical side of war. They appreciated the dramatic value of Dayan all the same, whose Hathaway-style black eyepatch and tough confidence became important symbols of Israeli faith and certainty.)

The three Israeli divisions started to roll into the Sinai amphitheater at 8:15 A.M., grinding through choking dust and ocher hills toward the greatest clash of tanks and armor ever seen. One brigade commander, who would not give his name because his young family lived in a border settlement exposed to reprisal raids, said: "My job is to penetrate Egyptian lines, and fan out behind, and attack them from the rear. A lot of Russian T–54 tanks have been buried in pits and are used as artillery, and the Egyptians are lacking in mobility. My men can run seven miles at a stretch, my entire force can keep going for four days on the water supplies we carry with us, and if our guns are not equal to the Russians', at least we've got a better reason to fight than the enemy. He can retreat. We can't."

General Yoffe said: "My division, an armored mobile division, has to penetrate through very difficult terrain which everyone will tell you is impossible, and to come to the rear of the enemy and try to do two things: stop reinforcements going in to the main defense, and try to catch anybody running away."

He did this by surging through slaglike sand dunes, to link up eventually with General Tal's forces. Tal, commanding tanks and armor, struck so fast across the formidable heart of the Sinai that there was a possibility at one stage of his men mistaking General Yoffe for the enemy and opening fire. "I can tell you it was a very dramatic moment," said Yoffe later, "standing there with the force, trying to coordinate matters so Tal in his momentum would not collide with my armor."

The mixed Israeli forces of American Sherman tanks, British Centurions and French AMX's, rumbled out of the Negev trailing field guns and half-track troop carriers. The coastal thrust toward the east end of the Gaza Strip was delayed by a belt of minefields and Egyptian trenches, and Israeli guns pounded the untidy barracks of the Palestine Liberation Army, whose leaders back in Cairo had boasted of retribution. The Liberation Army drew on some 700,000 Palestinian refugees, who came under fire too. Scattering, they joined the columns of lost and dazed Arabs who were soon to stumble blindly across the desert in search of water.

By nightfall the invaders of Gaza were shifting into the

high gear of night fighting, at which Israeli troops excelled. Other columns had sliced across the Sinai amphitheater, and by opening up the peninsula had performed the basic ground move on which the military planners had gambled. They had spread their remaining forces lightly along the Syrian and Jordanian fronts.

Everyone seemed sorry about the Kingdom of Jordan, which had joined Egypt at the last moment, and whose troops seized the UN building in Jerusalem, only to lose it after a brief but bitter battle. There was genuine regret for Jordan's folly even though, at this stage, the entry into the war of King Hussein's compact and well-trained forces could only create an unexpected new threat that Israel would have to properly deal with later. If Jordan's troops had struck from the poppy-covered hills of Amman during that first night, and if there had been any real quality of aggressiveness in Hussein's forces, matters might have gone differently for Israel. As it was, the Tel Aviv war room reflected the grim satisfaction of the field commanders and it seemed likely that the Israeli armies were actually moving ahead of their demanding timetable.

General Dayan had driven to Jerusalem to be sworn in as Defense Minister about eight hours after hostilities began. He found members of the Israeli Knesset, or parliament, preparing for a long session. They were like boisterous schoolchildren in their good humor, but he said later that none was in any doubt about the grave consequences of failure. Premier Eshkol held a cabinet meeting, Dayan raced back to the war room, and the Knesset decided to reject a suggestion that its evening session be held in the basement. Instead, the usual chamber was blacked out, and members held a soft-drink party in the anteroom. Many had never seen the Wailing Wall, more than two miles away across the battle zone, but all were confident it would soon be part of Israel's occupied territory.

Somehow the belief had established itself that Israel was already on the way to the most complete and shattering victory in history. Premier Eshkol expected Israeli troops to be at Sharm el Sheikh by the fourth day. He never dreamed that by the sixth *all* Israel's objectives would be gained: the Strait of Tiran, the Holy City, the west bank of the Jordan, the Suez Canal, and the Syrian heights where Arab artillery had bombarded Jewish settlements for so long that the world no longer cared.

CHAPTER SIX

In the name of Christianity we voice the fervent hope that in the unfortunate eventuality—which we firmly trust will never occur—that the situation may worsen, Jerusalem may, because of its peculiar sacred and holy character, be declared an open and inviolable city.

—Pope Paul, in a message to U Thant

Tuesday, June 6

In Cairo the war was a fantasy for the first 24 hours except for those directly hit by the first Israeli strikes. As if Arab propaganda had invented shadow conflicts for too long, the crowds chose to believe Nasser and the radio, and celebrated nonexistent victories. Ron Chester, in one of the last voice-casts to North America before Egyptian censors clamped down, told the CBC of cheering mobs and fantastic claims of Israeli planes shot down. One Egyptian report proved too unhappily true, however. An Israeli jet pilot, having ejected safely from his crippled plane, was hacked to bits by fellahin axes.

"Our people have been waiting 20 years for this battle!" cried Radio Cairo. "Arab armies have a rendezvous in Israel."

A chorus of abuse rose from other Arab capitals. "Kill the Jews!" cried Radio Baghdad. The sentiments were similar, the language only varying in degree, from Damascus to Amman.

For the first day at least, the Arab states had confused each other with claims of victories. Thus Jordan was wide open next morning for Israeli air strikes. King Hussein, it seemed, had believed Egypt's accounts of big air battles in which 86 Israeli jets fell to an Egyptian air force now dominating the skies. The massive self-deception practiced by the Arabs undoubtedly lost them any chance of recovering from Israel's surprise attacks. Indeed the make-believe war of Monday was exactly what Israel needed to camouflage her drive for territory she could hold before the UN arrived at a ceasefire plan. Egypt's best hope was to get Soviet-bloc allies in the UN to win a ceasefire on any terms, but the state radio continued unthinkingly to blare such announcements as: "The jihad, holy war, has started. Brother soldiers, your artillery has shot down 23 aircraft . . ."

Radio was vital to Israel's conduct of the war, and it was utilized with care and discretion. "We seemed to have transistors implanted in our heads," said a Jewish Agency girl. The announcements were cool and the music continued to be predominantly Jewish, with a few local hits by the High Winders and other Tel Aviv groups. Often the mothers and children sitting in air-raid shelters missed the All Clear because transistors were on full blast.

Once Radio Kol Israel experimented in some light fiction, stung by the outrageous claim from Cairo that 42 Israeli jets had just been destroyed. "Two Egyptian MIG–21's have shot each other down," said the Tel Aviv announcer in Arabic.

Jordan must have expected protection by Egyptian aircraft because the capital of Amman was stretched out defenseless when Israeli Mystère–IV's casually planted rockets and cannon shells around the city center soon after midnight. The radar station on the heights 20 miles north of Amman was destroyed earlier, but not before Jordanian operators claimed to have seen waves of aircraft rising out of the Mediterranean and banking toward Egypt. Although the operators could not have identified the planes (and their post at Ajlun was hidden behind the hills of Jordan's west bank), the report was to become the basis of an international incident. Desperate to explain away his defeat in the air, Nasser had broadcast on Tuesday at 4:37 A.M. over Cairo Radio this announcement: "It has been fully proved some British and U.S. aircraft are carrying out widescale activities in helping Israel."

Egypt's defeat in 1956 at the hands of the Israelis had always been blamed on Anglo-French air intervention, and thus Nasser had saved face. It seemed that he would seek refuge again in a similar claim, although this time there was no question of outside involvement. Israel had flattened the Arab air bases and her jets on this day took their time to drop bombs with pinpoint accuracy into pockets of Jordanian resistance.

King Hussein's legionnaires were yet to be forced to give up the Old City of Jerusalem. Israeli commandos encircled it at dawn. Other biblical towns were soon to be taken, as the Israeli forces moved into the kingdom west of the Jordan River and the Dead Sea. Jericho and Bethlehem, Hebron and Mount Scopus were falling into Israeli hands. The swift advance was again made possible by Israeli domination of the cloudless skies, and King Hussein seems to have been too flabbergasted to dissent from the Egyptian pretense of "an imperialist plot."

In Moscow a strange little scene was enacted. Murad Galeb, the Egyptian Ambassador, called a conference of Russian pressmen and played a tape of the Cairo Radio broadcast.

Many observers, having seen the Russians give full support to Egypt in earlier meetings of the Security Council, expected the worst. An ugly rumor like this one might bring Russian involvement, and a consequent reaction by the West. It was now an open secret that Russian technical advisors were working in large numbers with Syrian armed forces, and it seemed possible that Russia might be reluctant to suffer further humiliations—the destruction of her jets (including the new Sokhoi-7's) and the failure of her missiles were already an embarrassment.

Egypt's ruse did not work. The lie did not goad Russia into action. The desperate and unforgivably reckless invention by which Nasser and Hussein were apparently willing to risk a global holocaust did not succeed. Russian ships, hitherto regarded more as an irritant and even an impudence as they shadowed Anglo-American fleets, were suddenly a gift to the West; for they monitored Western air movements in the eastern Mediterranean and their own radar plots proved that no U.S. or British planes were involved.

Ambassador Galeb was received in stony silence by the Russian pressmen, who questioned him along lines that Premier Kosygin may have followed earlier. Apparently Galeb had gone straight to the Kremlin with the dangerous lie. He was asked how British planes could operate from the carriers Hermes and Victorious, the first of which was 1,500 miles from the war zone while the second was incapable of launching aircraft from her anchorage at Malta. As for the U.S. Sixth Fleet carriers, why had Russian ships seen no sign of aerial operations?

The canard was so dangerous that the Soviet censors let it

be known "the government finds no confirmation from other sources" and Moscow newspapers did not publish the report. The next day they did publish the fact that Arab diplomatic relations were being broken off with the U.S. and Britain for allegedly helping Israel, but the tone of the stories indicated Russian disinterest in exploiting this fact.

For once Israel's intelligence men, who are as close-mouthed as any, and perhaps more, shed some light upon their work. They released tapes of a radiophone conversation between President Nasser and King Hussein on this second day of war:

Nasser: How are you? The brother wants to know if the fighting is going on all along the front.

(The two leaders bellowed at each other, their voices apparently easy to identify.)

Nasser: Will His Majesty make an announcement on the participation of Americans and British?

(Answer not clear.)

Nasser: Hello, will we say the U.S. and England or just the U.S.?

Hussein: The U.S. and England.

Nasser: Does Britain have aircraft carriers . . . ?

(Answer not clear.)

Nasser: Good. King Hussein will make an announcement and I will make an announcement.

—Thank you.

—Do not give up.

—Yes.

Nasser: By God, I say that I will make an announcement and you will make an announcement and we will see to it that the Syrians will make an announcement that American and British airplanes are taking part against us from aircraft carriers. We will issue an announcement. We will stress the matter and we will drive the point home.

Hussein: Good. All right.

Nasser: A thousand thanks, don't give up, we are with you with all our heart and we are flying our planes over Israel today, our planes are striking at Israel's airfields since morning.

The tape recording was studied later by Western intelligence officers and its authenticity confirmed.* To back it up, British

* A "voiceprint" was made from a tape of the conversation by Lawrence G. Kersta, president of Voiceprint Laboratories in Somerville, New Jersey. The physicist worked all night on a recording transmitted from Tel Aviv by the Columbia Broadcasting System. He put it through

experts on the Jordan radar system released new details of the Ajlun post which supposedly detected the fleet of Anglo-American planes. The post was a Marconi–247 installation and it had been knocked out early in the war because it was more useful than two Arab radar units in the same region. Nevertheless, the Marconi–247 equipment was concealed from aircraft below 5,000 feet and closer than 50 miles; and so, in turn, aircraft outside a narrow corridor were hidden from the radar.

This was in many ways one of the more significant episodes of the war. It disclosed a maturity of behavior in the Russians that contrasted with their strongly pro-Egypt position in the UN; indeed, the inflexibility of the Soviet delegate, Dr. Nikolai Fedorenko, was to continue to startle radio and TV audiences in North America throughout the week. His voice was carried from the Security Council meetings on the air waves, and in translation he sounded ominously like some electronic robot, his words slow and deliberate, his manner ponderous. Again and again he attacked the Israeli representative, Gideon Rafael: "He has lied enough before this council," he intoned on one occasion. "It would be no great loss if he would generally refrain from any further statements here."

Nevertheless, the chill had gone out of such flat Russian statements. Only 72 hours earlier Peter Woods of the BBC, an experienced commentator with a good deal of experience at the UN, had gloomily pondered the probable Russian response to just the kind of situation that Nasser was now trying to manufacture. Sitting in his room at the Tel Aviv Hilton, he reviewed the known strength of Russian forces in the Mediterranean. "There's an awful symmetry to the whole picture," he muttered. "The cradle near Jerusalem could be our grave."

an electronic filtering process to eliminate interference in the radiophone link between Cairo and Amman and eventually obtained a "pure" sample of what the two leaders were alleged to have said. A State Department official from Washington who spoke Arabic was present during the tests which, said Kersta, left him "100 per cent sure that this is the voice of President Nasser." The Kersta technique has been used in evidence in U.S. courts and is called "voiceprint identification." It is based on the principle that each individual has a voice as distinctively identifiable as a fingerprint. The method does not try to understand words. Instead when a word is uttered it appears as a visual pattern on a spectograph. An activated stylus converts this to vertical lines on a revolving drum and the position of the lines along a vertical scale reflects the frequency of the sound and their darkness reflects the volume. The space between the first and last line indicates the speed of speech. Kersta said physical differences such as in nasal cavities produce a basic and distinctive sound for each individual. Recordings of Nasser's voice on other occasions were used for comparison. It should be added Kersta's methods have been challenged by some scientists, who complain they are too imprecise.

Now the prospects had undergone a startling change. The Russians were found to be urbane and just as anxious to restore peace; and while Dr. Fedorenko plodded through his predictable speeches, there was some swift "hot-line" conversation between Washington and Moscow later this Tuesday. It became apparent that Israeli victories made it imperative that a ceasefire be imposed before the Jewish armies were spread all over the Mideast. Thus the ruse by Egypt to sharpen the antagonism between Russia and the West would have been disastrous to Arab interests if it had worked, for the most important goal now was to halt the fighting and freeze the Israeli armored columns in their tracks.

The disclosure of the Nasser-Hussein conversation also made it clear that Israel was in possession of a remarkably efficient security organization. This had been apparent for a long time to those with a professional interest in such matters. It came as a surprise to those who regarded the Jews as just about the gabbiest people on earth. "We don't conceal anything," a government spokesman said ruefully. "If we run out of dirty washing, there's always someone else's to hang out in public." Yet it had required an exceptional secretiveness among thousands of ordinary people to conceal all the preparations for this unwanted war.

In Jerusalem, where gloomy prophets had imagined humanity's grave, the sacred Old City now presented an extraordinary spectacle.

> Palestine is the center of the world.
> Jerusalem is the center of Palestine.
> The Temple is the center of Jerusalem.
> The Holy of Holies is the center of the Temple.
> The Ark is the center of the Holy of Holies.
> In the center of the Ark rests the stone called "The Foundation Stone of the World."

The site of the Temple had been denied to Jews for nearly 2,000 years and if they occasionally had access to it, this was by permission of indulgent conquerors. The geometric metaphor of a Jewish scholar (above) fixed in words the sense of awe with which the sanctuary built by Moses has been always regarded, a repository for the stone Tables of the Testimony—the Ten Commandments.

Suddenly the Old Walled City became a target of mystical significance. Inside were the holy sites that inspired three of the world's great religious movements: Moslems and Christians as well as Jews. A citizen army of Israelis began to converge upon it. They wore odds and ends of clothing. Some had tin helmets and some had Jewish skullcaps. Some arrived in Tel Aviv buses. Their ammunition wagons were farm carts hauled by tractors, wooden-sided trucks, mud-caked fiberglass station wagons.

Their resolve was strengthened by the pasting Jordan's guns had given the Israeli sector of the divided city of Jerusalem. In response to Egypt's call for "a second front," King Hussein's legionnaires began to lob mortar and artillery shells into the grounds of the King David Hotel and the back yards around Premier Eshkol's home.

Three shells smashed some of the stained-glass windows in the Hadassah Medical Center's synagogue. The windows were the work of Marc Chagall, who wrote from France: "I am not worried about the windows, only about the safety of Israel. Let Israel be safe and I will make you lovelier windows."

The message was typical of many pouring into Jerusalem from around the world. "It was almost worth the shelling," said former Israeli Foreign Minister Mrs. Golda Meir, "to know how much love existed for us." Then she shook her head sadly, saying that even the loss of one life was never worth such a reassurance. Her reaction was typical. Even later, in victory, the people of Israel showed no desire to celebrate; and only deplored the unavoidable loss of life. In Jerusalem early reports spoke of 500 dead and wounded. The Isaiah Scroll, the most complete of the Dead Sea Scrolls, was placed in an underground vault with other precious relics. Meanwhile Israeli commando units prowled to the edge of the Old City and planned an assault, to be conducted only with small-arms and in such a way that the holy places would escape damage.

Snipers of the royal Jordan army concealed themselves in minarets, in the Monastery of Flagellation, above the Gates of St. Stephen and Damascus, and in Solomon's Stables. They were almost the only Arab regulars left within the Old City when night fell.

"An Arab Legion battalion captured Government House, and this started the action," Colonel Eliezer Amitai, the Jerusalem brigadier commander, told me. "There'd been firing of a type we were not accustomed to breaking out all along the Arab line, and the entire city was shelled including my command post.

56

"I mounted a counterattack from the direction of the Experimental Farm and we took Government House after heavy fighting. There were about 100 UN personnel in Government House, and they asked to be taken out into Jordan, which was interesting." The colonel paused, sucking the tip of his pencil reflectively. "We continued our attack. Our main problems were the positions known as SAUSAGE, linking Government House with Sur-Bahar, and BELL inside Sur-Bahar proper. I wanted to take these and at the same time decisively defeat the Arab Legion, which in the past refused to recognize we were competent to hurt them if necessary. [The Legionnaires had kept up terrorist raids in the belief that Israel was too soft to retaliate.] By nightfall this was done, but it was only at the end of the operation that I learned the officer commanding the regiment had been hit first at Government House and then again at Sur-Bahar, but insisted on fighting on.

"Heavy shelling continued throughout the night, and in the early hours of Tuesday Colonel Gur joined me with his brigade of paratroopers, who fought all through Tuesday toward the Rockefeller Museum. My troops attacked the quarter overlooking the railway station—Abu Tor—and we lost the regiment commander. The Legionnaires did not run easily and fought from house to house through narrow crooked streets. By night we had thrown them back and were descending to the Kidron Valley.

"Gur began the attack on the Old City as we advanced on Mount Zion on Wednesday. We cleared the southern section of the Weeping Wall on the outer side so that Gur and his men, fighting inside the Old City, had at least this much relief. The logical next step, in the overall action, I guessed to be attacks in Bethlehem and Hebron, and so it was. We received our orders to attack battle positions at Mar Elias and at 2:00 P.M. this action began. I advanced with a small armored group, my infantry regiments speeding along behind me as fast as they could to Bethlehem.

"I ought to mention," said Colonel Amitai in the same matter-of-fact voice, "one of my commanders was killed inside an Arab house when Legionnaires jumped his men with knives."

In Sinai the campaign was by this second day swinging into that magic rhythm described by field commanders as "getting your tail up." The tank armadas were locking guns. The expensive monsters should have maneuvered like ships of the line, but the Egyptians in their gigantic Soviet T–55's seemed hypnotized into aiming their 100-mm guns at "the enemy to the north," and they were exposed to attack from the rear like overturned armadillos offering their soft underbellies to a voracious enemy.

Israel Tal was a wiry little Galilean with the oblong face of a cocky Mediterranean beachcomber: quizzical mouth, cynical brown eyes, and a disrespect for authority. He was, all the same, commanding armor. Like other field commanders, he led his men. "There is no order in this army like 'forward,' " he said. "Officers say only 'follow me.' " In cold print that sounds like bravado but Brigadier-General Tal was not a boastful man. On foot he moved with the peculiar heel-and-toe stride of a desert commando, and when he talked he rested hands on hips and stared at his questioner with a face innocent of expression and eyes that never flickered. He was 43 when he got command of the division that was to smash through the fortified lines of the Egyptian First Division, reinforced by the Palestine Liberation Brigade.

"Our main purpose was to destroy the enemy's divisions," he said later, "and not to occupy as much territory as possible. We knew the first breakthrough action at Rafah (west of Gaza along the coast road) would be the first actual trial of strength between us and the Egyptian army which we had not fought for ten years."

He wiped the back of a farmer's hand across his bronzed face. "It was clear to all our soldiers and officers that the action would therefore be carried out regardless of losses."

Perhaps the fiercest tank battle of the war developed on this second day when Tal's armor burst through concrete Arab fortifications and reached El Arish without waiting for the support vehicles. Arab forces reorganized and for a time Tal's tanks were cut off. "We launched a night attack with mechanized infantry," said Tal, "and the whole division cut its way through to El Arish where a prolonged tank battle took place around the airbase . . . We destroyed a hundred tanks on the field, and hundreds of cannon."

(The charred tanks and sun-split Egyptian bodies were still there a week later when buses took newsmen through the carnage. The tanks carried the manufacturer's label: Gorkisky Autozavod. The dead lay as they had fallen. Their bodies had swollen in the heat, the flesh peeled back already, the legs and arms stiff like toothpicks in new boiled potatoes.)

58

The statue of a Palestinian soldier, pointing to Israel ("his homeland," said the inscription) was blown apart in Gaza by one of Tal's tanks. It must have been about this time that nine Indian members of UNEF, a Brazilian member, and an Irish UN observer were killed.

For the first time, a note of realism crept into Egyptian army communiqués. Israel forces were reported to have penetrated Egyptian territory, but this was not reported on Cairo Radio. Instead, Arab broadcasts continued to speak of a valiant opposition to enemy [Israeli] attacks in which "a gigantic air force has been thrown." Egyptian listeners were told that scores of Israeli settlements had been shelled, scores of Israeli planes shot down, while their armies were striking deep into Israel's heartland. Jordan's official radio proclaimed: "What is hap-

SECOND DAY
JUNE 6

LEBANON — O Damascus

SYRIA

ISRAEL

Mediterranean Sea

Jordan R.

Tel Aviv

Amman

Gaza

Jerusalem

Port Said

El Arish

SUEZ CANAL

Abu Aweigila

Ismailia

El Quseima

JORDAN

Cairo

Kuntilla

U.A.R.

SINAI PENINSULA

Gulf of Suez

Gulf of Aqaba

Nile River

Sharm el Sheik

SAÚDI ARABIA

Strait of Tiran

Israeli forces

Red Sea

0   MI.   100

pening in Jerusalem is a holy war for the Ka'aba, for Mohammed, and the Holy Koran tells us there will be a welcome in a Paradise for those who fall."

What was about to happen in Jerusalem must have severely shaken Arab confidence in this interpretation of Paradise.

CHAPTER SEVEN

And God spake unto Israel, in the visions
of the night, and said . . . "Fear not to go down
in Egypt, for I will there make of thee a great
nation. I will go down with thee into Egypt
and I will also surely bring thee up again.
> —Genesis 46:2-6

Wednesday, June 7

The people of Israel fought their way to the Wailing Wall in the Old City of Jerusalem from dawn to noon. There was an assault battalion of the 1st Jerusalem Regiment and there were Sherman tanks. There were girl-soldiers with FN 7.62-mm automatics, and there were elderly veterans from other wars— a London cockney with a load of six mortar bombs; a Russian rabbi with an Uzzi submachine gun, in which he took an unholy joy. The thump of cannon shook the nearby Vale of Hinnom and rolled along the slopes of Mount Zion. Smoke lifted above the Garden of Gethsemane and the road to Bethlehem shook under the tracks of a blindly probing tank.

The Wailing Wall was regained at a time when Egyptian forces in Sinai discovered how dreadful a predicament they were in. Their armor was trapped at the mouth of the Mitla Pass; the tanks of Israel were jerking across their rear along the Suez Canal; the garrison of Sharm-el-Sheikh, where all the trouble had started was scrambling to escape from Israeli paratroops; and in the Gaza Strip the dupes of the Palestine Liberation Army, with their cans of Red Chinese ham and their Arabic versions of Mao Tse-tung's Thoughts, were huddled under a rain of mortars among the orange groves following the fall of the city of Gaza.

On every hand the Arab now reeled under the impact of guns and jets. What had been a seeming disadvantage, the small size of David, proved now to be his strength. His lines of communication were short, his power compressed. His foes sprawled to east, west and south, bewildered in defeat and too widely scattered to muster their strength—which on paper was still formidable.

It seemed appropriate that, in such an hour, the Jewish generals should join their troops under the Wailing Wall to the sound of a ram's horn.

What remained of the Wall was about 100 feet long, and weeds and bits of shrub grew in the cracks. It had been the outer wall of Solomon's Temple, according to the Jewish poet Agnon, "left by the Almighty in His infinite mercy to symbolize the Twelve Tribes. Each Jew may direct his thoughts according to his height at his stone. It is built of huge stones, each one five ells by six ells. No structure in the world has such stones, and they live together without any kind of plaster holding them together, like the Jewish people, which has no government to hold it together yet is one united entity."

To this place, generation upon generation of Jews had come, seeking to sing their prayers for the lost state of Judea. But always the Wall was in other hands, and to weep beneath it was not a right but a privilege extended by others. This had been so since the time when the Romans had destroyed Judea and erected in the sanctuary great temples to their own gods of Venus and Bacchus.

Platoons of Jewish soldiers were moving between small twisted trees and shrubs around Mount Zion, as the Arab Legion opened with automatic fire above the Franciscan Church. Along the Damascus road lumbered a troop of three Sherman tanks in support of an assault on the Dung Gate. Some of the scrubland around the Old City was burning from mortar fire, and the air was hot and dry.

The first infantry through the Gate located the Wall from the blue and gold dome of the Mosque of Omar behind it. The hot narrow streets were covered by Jordanian snipers, and the sharp whine of their bullets was more startling than the steady crump of mortars and the echoing staccato of the Uzzi submachine guns.

There must have been a great deal of nervous excitement. Eyewitnesses later described how men were shot, sometimes by

62

their own guns, as they ran toward the Wall in a state of religious exaltation. The slopes below the Old City were littered with bodies, some of them unmarked, including women and children killed by concussion.

The Arab legionnaires were flushed from positions around the Wall with utmost difficulty. Israeli soldiers fired first and asked their questions later. A young corporal had found a blue and white cloth which he wrapped around his shoulders as a prayer shawl. No longer conscious of enemy fire, he leaned against the Wall and cradled his head in his bent elbow. His submachine gun thrust its snout up under the shawl so that he appeared to stand there with some monstrous growth in his back, his body rocking gently in prayer.

"I suppose like other Jews I've unconsciously waited for this day," said another soldier, David Kohn, a Jerusalem butcher in normal times. "I don't remember the last part, before I got to the Wall. My last memory is an Arab bazooka blowing open a door, and then I was leaning my head against the Wall and it has that smell, you know, very old and—comforting."

The men kept coming, some bleeding from wounds, some supporting their injured comrades, some wiping the sweat from their faces, and some openly weeping.

"There were six million of us," said Colonel Jacob Gillon, gray with fatigue, a survivor from Auschwitz. He said it without self-consciousness. "I seemed to burst with all their tears."

The streets were lined with Arab prisoners, hands above heads. Israeli soldiers kept pouring across the Mosque of Omar square, looking for the Wailing Wall. They covered their heads with handkerchiefs, newspapers—anything that served as a proper headpiece, and stood before the ancient stones with a strangely absorbed look in their eyes "as if," wrote one observer "they had suddenly withdrawn from the noisy world around them." Many non-Jews who saw them began to comprehend the consuming love and the fierce sense of protection they felt for the city. There was no question that the Israeli army had sustained heavier casualties than necessary because of their concern for the holy places, and a senior officer told Gerald Clark of the *Montreal Star*: "They were anxious not to repeat the unfortunate incident at Monte Cassino in Italy during World War II." The authorities were reluctant to let the world know what damage had been done. The

12th-century church of Saint Anne was badly wrecked, and the great wooden doors of the Al Aksa Mosque were smashed to matchwood, but these might have been victims of Arab artillery since there was no evidence that Israel's forces used heavy arms of any kind. Instead they had captured the hills ringing the city first. The battle had taken place—the real fighting in which men had slammed into each other with weapons of destruction, on the rim of Jerusalem which remained at the center, an assembly of medieval domes and towers and walls, like a woodcut from some ancient volume.

The giant stones of the Wall were what many soldiers first remembered in retrospect. And the sudden realization that they were here; that on this hot day, with the sky filled with smoke and events moving so quickly that they had stumbled upon this hour without adequate preparation, that here and now they were witnesses of an event that would take its place among the legends. Here Solomon had built the Temple. This had been the wall erected by poor laborers, and here the Divine Presence had said, "The toil of the poor is precious in My eyes and My blessing shall be upon it." Here, said the legends, stones had been laid by Abraham and Isaac, Jacob and Joseph, David and Solomon.

"Blessed is the Lord," prayed the soldiers on this day. "Blessed is the King of the Universe who kept us in life and sustained us and enabled us to reach this time."

Also, on this third day, the noonday sun blazed down upon the baked flat stones of the desert where the Russian tanks squatted like giant boulders and the MIGs hugged the sand with smashed wings. General Tal's forces had joined those of General Yoffe during the night, and several hundred Israeli tanks formed an iron wall blocking the escape of the Egyptians toward Suez. "An attempt to pull our 'cork' out of the bottleneck at Bir Gifgafa was made by Arab T–55 tanks," Tal said later. "We had positioned a regiment of light French AMX tanks, which engaged about sixty enemy tanks in a two-hour battle to prevent the Arab relief forces breaking through."

The Soviet T–55s carried 100–mm guns against the Israeli 75–mm's mounted in the AMXs, but the terrain was such that Jewish armor scuttled around and behind the enemy. The Egyptians were faithful to their textbooks and failed to see that —in the Sinai especially—a formation of tanks should be navigated like a fleet at sea; that an attack could come from

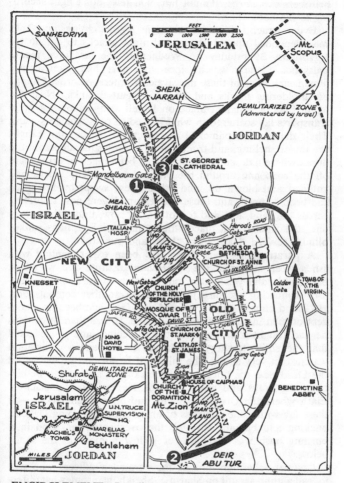

ENCIRCLEMENT: Israelis said they had surrounded the Jordanian sector of Jerusalem in a pincers movement (1 and 2) and seized area around Mount Scopus (3).

any quarter at any time. As General Tal later expressed it: "We literally smote them hip and thigh. I heard later some prisoners explained: 'It's not fair, you Jews don't fight according to the book.'"

Every Israeli soldier is trained in night fighting, and Tal's men depended upon surprise and night attacks to cut up the Egyptians. By midday on Wednesday the air force reconnaissance planes, which since the start had meticulously filmed each stage of these massive encounters, recorded clumps of smoldering trucks and dumps of gutted tanks. Near the Mitla Pass, a poignant place on Israeli army maps, Egyptian transports lay scattered in what looked to be a wreckers' yard. Their drivers had panicked as leaders in the column caught fire under shelling, and trucks stood at grotesque angles on the dunes where a desperate attempt had been made to drive them off the road and around the blocked traffic. The trucks had collided and blown up, and others were swept by fire. Men had been trapped, and those who escaped were now stumbling across the sand, lost and forgotten. By now, under the savage sun, the Sinai was a place where unarmed Egyptians stalked blindly toward death from thirst and sunstroke.

A paratroop reservist, who had been experimenting with fish a week earlier at the Weizmann Institute and would be back in his lab a week later, looked down on the scene preparatory to making his third jump into yet another combat zone. He found himself again aware of why God had become a concept of men in such a fierce landscape. In less than three days he had fought over much of the Bibleland, and he reflected that the entire territory which had so influenced civilization was in fact very small. The pillars of basalt and sandstone on the Dead Sea, the unreal brightness of the star above Bethlehem, the crags and craters of the Negev and the place at Elath where the Queen of Sheba had once disembarked—all these lay within the compass of an oil-smeared, aging Dakota, bucking and banging through the overheated air. God in a burning bush was the blaze of yellow mimosa in the sands below.

Colonel Scherman, one of the paratroop officers who was to lead a jump assault on Sharm-el-Sheikh, had somewhat different thoughts. Before the campaign began, sitting in his peaceful suburban home outside Tel Aviv, he had talked of what it was like to emerge from the Nazi extermination camps as the only child to survive in a family of ten; and soberly he said, "This time, if I have to fight the same enemies, I shall have a weapon in my hand, and my own country to defend." He was a big man, slow and purposeful, and he had known the war was coming. "I smell it," he said, and ten days before the jump assault he dug a trench in his back yard, and his son and daughter lined it with bags filled with sand.

The paratroops were made up of volunteers, trained in all the deadly arts, fussed over by men who had learned from Orde Wingate to fight with unconventional weapons, to strike when the enemy slept, to kill swiftly and silently. During this campaign they were moved from one end of Israel to another in a continuous shuttle. They arrived over Sharm-el-Sheikh to find their navy had got there first. The Egyptians had fled. For old soldiers like Colonel Scherman it was a moment to be thankful. He had seen violent death on too many occasions, and he no longer suffered the sense of let-down that sometimes afflicts men who are screwed up for combat. Instead, he organized a caravan of water-carrying trucks to rescue some of the dazed Egyptian soldiers he had seen trudging across the Sinai moonscape.

By noon, a full report of the tank battle along the East-West axis between Beersheba and the Mitla Pass overlooking Suez was available in the Tel Aviv war room. It surprised even the most optimistic commanders, for it recorded a speed of advance never before achieved by armor. The headquarters of the Egyptian forces in Sinai had cracked apart, and the Israeli columns could be expected to snake south from three points along the Canal to complete their capture of the peninsula.

Trying to explain this swift success, Ariel Sharon, the paratroop Brigadier-General, described a typical battle: "We operated many troops together—armor, paratroops, infantry, artillery, engineers. At this particular point the enemy had an infantry brigade and about 90 tanks, with 6 regiments of artillery. We opened the attack with paratroops who fell upon the Egyptian artillery from the rear. Then our infantry made a frontal assault, while tanks penetrated the enemy line to the north and attacked from the rear. With our tanks behind them and our armored troops now hitting them from the front, the enemy was trapped. The fighting began in the evening at 10:30 and continued until six the next morning. We

67

came under very heavy artillery fire and opened a path for another division to join us and move through us."

Ariel Sharon grinned suddenly. "I'm very much afraid we are all going to be too old for the next war. We completed this one in such a way that the enemy is not going to fight for many, many years to come."

The Sinai victory was colossal in its implications. "We have inflicted almost total destruction on the Egyptian army," said Major-General Yitzhak Rabin. It had been the object of the campaign to smash as much Arab might as possible before the cumbersome machinery of UN peacemaking could move into action. Thus the Israeli field commanders had been tensed for a different operation than the 1956 battles which had made General Dayan famous. Instead of a thrust to the center and south, the mobile armor divisions seized the three natural routes to Suez and trapped the bulk of Egyptian forces between.

This masterpiece of politico-military planning made itself suddenly evident to the Russians. Their reaction was swift. Startled delegates to the UN saw Dr. Fedorenko perform a sharp diplomatic turnabout. Two weeks earlier he had opposed the calling of a Security Council emergency meeting, declaring that there was nothing in the Mideast situation to warrant it. And he continued to play an obstructive role, followed by other Communist delegates and their friends. Now, he urgently presented a resolution calling for an absolute cease-fire by 1600 hours GMT.

The motive was clear enough. Moscow wanted to stop the dreadful destruction of Egyptian forces. The hundred and ten million Arabs from the Atlantic to the Persian Gulf were watching a brutal demonstration of Russian weakness. The best of Russian arms were being smashed by inferior weapons, and Russia was powerless to help her Egyptian ally against a tiny foe.

Meanwhile, in Jerusalem, the conviction grew that Israel had won such a victory that it must compare with the defeat of the Armada, in its symbolism and vast implications. The Jews are not, however, a martial people. There was none of the tipsy self-congratulation of a conquering army. "To our Arab neighbors," said General Dayan, "we extend, and with added emphasis at this hour, our hand in peace. To Christian and Moslem we solemnly promise full religious freedom and rights. We do not come to Jerusalem for the sake of other people's holy places but in order to safeguard its entirety."

The capture of the Old City now presented fresh military problems, however, none of them entirely disagreeable to a citizens' army which had seen its border settlements under the threat of the bully boys next door. The Jordan troops had been forced south to group in static defensive positions. The open west bank of the Jordan was always a potential danger to Israel. Despite his many preoccupations on other fronts, General Dayan could not permit Jordan's forces to go unpunished. "Look at the map," he said, "and see what it means to have artillery fire directed at Israel from Jordan. . . . I cannot say why Jordan started to attack us. . . . A few days ago two Egyptian commando battalions were transferred to Jordan, and Jordanian forces are under the command of an Egyptian general."

Early on Wednesday a sufficient number of Israeli troops were available to attack the heights of Nablus where Jordan's artillery had shelled as far as Tel Aviv.

They faced an unpleasant task. King Hussein's troops were regarded as the best trained in the Arab world. In an English garden in Sussex, the man who was most responsible for shaping them into an efficient fighting force—Sir John Glubb—had said: "They're hardy hill people and they make great fighting men. They remind me of the Highland clans of Scotland." He sounded strangely out of touch with present events, and a report of his views in the *Jerusalem Post* reminded readers how much the Middle East had changed since he had commanded the Arab Legion and for 17 years was known as Glubb Pasha—romantic echo of an age when Englishmen and bedouin roamed the desert together.

Under King Hussein, the forces of Jordan could prove a dangerous ally of Egypt. And it was known that one Arab plan called for strikes across Israel from two sides: from the Egypt positions in Sinai and from Jordan, cutting the Jewish state in three.

"We would have been sliced up pretty thin," said David Ben-Gurion, after visiting the Wailing Wall that day. His house in Tel Aviv was only 12 miles from the Jordan border as the shell flies.

There was a possibility that Jordanian troops might charge down the road from Nablus, west through Qualqiliya, to take

69

Tel Aviv. To forestall such a move, an Israeli force had already taken the vital road junction of Jenin, north of Nablus.

This force typified the flexible, long-range units which Israel had developed under the direction of veterans of desert warfare. These men, mostly in their mid-forties, had learned from General Wingate—then a young British Army captain—to take terrifying gambles, to throw away the army manuals, to strike without regard for convention, to cherish no odd notions of chivalry when a struggle was to the death, and to place emphasis upon originality, surprise and mobility. As a result, the Israeli army always baffled the military analysts because its composition was never clear. Its units formed and re-formed in accordance with the needs of the day. Field commanders had great freedom of decision.

Girl soldiers who served with such units were lean and tough as saplings. Every man was a fighting unit in himself, and there was no nonsense about soldiers serving only as cooks, or batmen, or in the supply lines. Their equipment might include 50-ton British Centurion tanks and heavy artillery, armed with American "Priest" 105–mm self-propelled Howitzers mounted on a 25-ton Sherman chassis. They had half-track troop carriers, light AMX–13 tanks and bulldozer tanks, but you could never be sure. As the Tank Commander General Tal had said: "All our equipment is getting old and, we improvise all the time."

On the occasion of Jordan's defeat, ironically, these guerillalike forces accomplished a textbook demonstration of almost Roman classicism in the use of the pincer movement. A two-prong attack on Jenin had opened the northern Jordan front, and early on Wednesday the Israeli forces began to close about the Nablus heights.

The subsequent use of tactical air power will undoubtedly provide material for military historians for a long time to come. For 18 hours the Israeli air force discharged wave after wave of fighter-bombers to rake the Nablus ridge and the Jordan valley with rockets and napalm. On Wednesday afternoon four Israeli armored columns broke into Nablus and found a third of King Hussein's army of 55,000 men injured, or dead, or running.

"Kill the Jews wherever you find them," King Hussein said in a broadcast at 12:15 P.M. on Wednesday. "Kill them with your arms, with your hands, with your nails and teeth." Shortly

70

strength, had pressed the Security Council all the time into ...
action on ..... to ..... the situation. That was the task
of the Israeli .... Israel was in ..... since midnight
..... and Israel realized he should hold firm.
... now had essentially points for three days, and the
Egyptians, on whom each day .... had to ... abide by any
agreement to separate .... from the .... preparations for the war
book. He had in a thousand other ways .... After

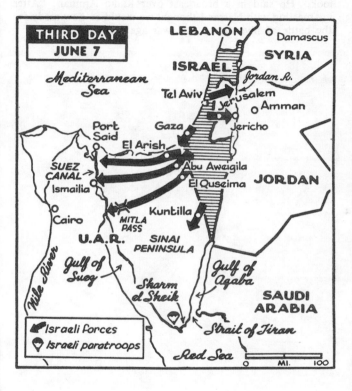

71

afterward he grasped the Security Council call for a ceasefire as the only means of saving his kingdom. There was no more talk of "the Legion's artillery destroying Jerusalem completely," and Jordan grabbed the chance for a truce.

"I have been continually awake for three days," said the 32-year-old monarch next day. "Do not be misled by my appearance to suppose there is any other reason for the way I look." He said in a broadcast over Radio Amman: "After my meeting with Nasser I thought we would be now ready for the battle of liberation . . . I was again let down."

CHAPTER EIGHT

Citizens of Jerusalem! You have proved worthy inhabitants of the City of David. You have proved worthy of the words of the Psalmist: If I forget thee, O Jerusalem, may my right hand forget its cunning.
—Message from Teddy Kollek,
Mayor of Jerusalem

Thursday, June 8

The Chief Rabbis of Israel and the Army had arrived at the Wailing Wall the previous day with the deliberately unglamorous figure of Premier Levi Eshkol, who had shaken every soldier in sight by the hand, murmuring, "Kinderlach, little ones." He was a Ukrainian Jew, with the quiet intellectualism of the East European, and his appearance seemed to confirm that civic authority had taken charge. "Tell them all may worship in this city," Eshkol told a foreign correspondent. "Tell them this city will be open to all. Tell them that."

A son of the Chief Rabbi of Dublin was busy on the west bank of Jordan trying to restore order and public services. He was General Vivian Herzoz, a former British army officer of the Black Watch, who had broadcast throughout the war a daily analysis of the battles exploding on every front. On his hands were thousands of Arab refugees. In Tel Aviv a government official said that if Israel were to assimilate the million Arabs who came under her rule with the conquest of the Gaza Strip and the western part of Jordan, there could be an Arab majority there by the first decade of the next century.

The Mandelbaum Gate, so long a depressing exit from Jerusalem into no-man's land, saw the assembly of devout Jews in long black coats and black hats.

The pale white light that always shines upon Jerusalem must have seemed to contain a special quality to those who had listened for 19 years to the crack of guns on the northern shore of Galilee. All around, places that were thought to be permanently in Arab hands were now free: Jericho, nestling in its green valley beyond Judea; Bethlehem five miles away on a burnt hill deep inside what had once been Jordan.

The Hebrew name of the holy city is "Yerushalayim," which means City of Peace. On this remarkable day, with clouds chasing across the sky, and Jacob's Ladders playing like spotlights on smoking tanks or a ruined crusader's castle, a time of new miracles might have seemed at hand. Even in taking the Old City the Israeli troops had accomplished a miraculous operation, seeking to avoid injury to the shrines of other faiths.

Some young reservists arrived in double-deck red buses, big swaying Leylands that seemed to come straight off the London streets. Others squatted in kibbutz trucks. Many vehicles were painted in vivid colors with advertisements for laundries and bakeries and soft drinks. One van bore the bold inscription: THREE WISE MEN DEPARTMENT STORE—BETHLEHEM. Their vehicles were smeared in mud which provided an effective camouflage, rather in the way that an elephant in East Africa becomes impregnated with ochre soil until he looks like an earthen mound. Every Israeli unit carried its own pot of white paint to mark captured transport.

The first Arab tanks had been knocked out below the Mount of Olives. After a column of Israeli armor poked cautiously up the road, a Star of David broke from the hilltop and Israeli troops jumped onto buses and went riding off to Mount Scopus, laughing and singing, although enemy fire still crackled around them.

A crew of Jordanian gunners sat in the valley of Jehosophat and pumped shells at the French Mission of Nazareth. Nuns in white smocks, with crosses painted in Mercurochrome, worked among bodies with limbs flung into positions that would have been impossible in life.

The Israeli bus cooperative, Hamkasher, restored the Number 9 bus service to Mount Scopus for the first time since the last run in 1948. The driver was the son of the man killed at its wheel in 1948, and the number had been reserved for the day the run could be resumed. This sentimental gesture was a reminder that the loss of Mount Scopus (one of the eastern

74

hills left inside Jordan) had been almost as bad as the loss of the Wailing Wall. The truce terms had made it clear that Israelis were to have access to the Hebrew University on Scopus, but in practice the Jordanians had permitted only a ceremonial visit twice a month, and eventually a new university had to be built. It rose on Givat Ram, a hill above the western edge of the city, another creative result of the struggle imposed by Arab enmity. And so the ancient Number 9 bus struggling back to Scopus was a symbol of victory more meaningful than a clutch of military bulletins.

These continued to report the progress of the war in sober tones. The mood of celebration in Jerusalem, the talk of cease-fires, was misleading. The Egyptians were still trying to blast a passage out of the Sinai trap. Egyptian jets flew on what amounted to *kamikaze* missions. There was still Syria to deal with, whose armies had failed to match the bloodthirsty threats of Radio Damascus with any decisive action.

There was uneasiness when bulldozers began to sweep away the Arab hovels clustering near the Wailing Wall. The army had decided to clear a square to accommodate the pilgrims who reached the staggering total of 350,000 soon after the war ended.

But even if the authorities had wanted to dampen the fervor caused by the Wall, they were overwhelmed by the emotional crowds. Even General Dayan was caught up in the ecstasy of the moment and said: "We felt we were fighting to prevent the fall of the Third Temple." The Wall, of course, was a surviving piece of Solomon's 10th Century B.C. Second Temple.

The bulldozing of Arab homes, said a Hebrew scholar, was unfortunate but not surprising. "Here lived the Arab Grand Mufti of Jerusalem. He stirred up riots in the 1920's and 1930's. He accused Jews of ritually murdering Christian children and said we tortured domestic animals. He backed Hitler and his hatred was the inspiration of many Arab leaders today. So don't expect us to behave impeccably all the time."

All over the country, the more orthodox Jews were talking of a new Messiah heralded by the return to the Wall. Many believed he would appear on Wednesday, June 14, the Festival of the Giving of the Tora (*Shavuot*) which is the traditional birthday and death anniversary of King David. On that day thousands of Jews walked along the four-and-a-half kilometers to Mount Zion through the Dung Gate and back through the Armenian Quarter to Jaffa Gate. Mothers pushed children in prams and youths supported graybearded parents come to take a last look at the Wall they had never before seen. Hundreds spent all night around Mount Zion, praying.

"For almost 20 years the Jordan government failed to honor its guarantee under the Armistice Agreement to permit the people of Israel access to the Western Wall," observed the *Jerusalem Post* that same day. "To be cut off from this physical link with the nation's past was [a form of] exile. For centuries the Wall has been a place of pilgrimage to Jews. This tradition was renewed yesterday with an enthusiasm and fervor as must have astonished even those who were aware that these great blocks of stone have acquired a national symbolism quite unmatched in Jewish life . . . *If there was anyone here or elsewhere who still had any shadow of doubt concerning the future of Jerusalem, yesterday's pilgrimage provided the answer: Under no circumstances, whatever the pressures may be, will the citizens of Israel allow anyone to cut them off again from the Wall which stands at the center of their city and is the essence and reason for its existence.*"

Meanwhile the strange and terrible pilgrimage back to Egypt was beginning to make an impression on the Suez Canal ports. Passengers on a liner traveling through the Canal were horrified to see tattered skeletons of men wandering dazedly through Port Said, Ismailia and Suez. "They looked like broken dolls," said Beverly Johnstone of Boston, Mass. "Some were covered from head to foot in blisters. I saw one man with an arm dangling, and blood congealed on his face and bare legs, fall like a ninepin. Almost all the men were covered head to foot in light sand and they looked like ghosts."

There was no evidence that Egypt, which was complaining about alleged Israeli indifference to the defeated troops, had prepared for their reception. "They just wandered off down the streets with their arms stretched out," said Lt. Joseph Lucas, a British Army officer on one of the ships. "Against the bare landscape they looked bigger than life and they come over the dunes, and there we were, lounging on the ship's rail, and it seemed the most awful confrontation. It was like Exodus in reverse."

This generally blurred impression of war overlapping into peace was reported from Sinai, where some of the hardest fighting was in progress even while local residents in Ashkelon, near the Gaza Strip, gossiped in sidewalk cafés over their coffee and apfelstrüdel.

The aim of Israel's armor spearheads and attack-squadrons of Mirage–3 C's was to crush as much Egyptian power as possible in the small time that remained, to cripple militant Arab resolve with a final thunderous onslaught upon every Russian-equipped unit which could be turned into a legitimate target. Israeli tanks and infantry held the Egyptian side of the north-south ridge on the Suez flank of the Sinai peninsula; but instead of taking the Canal they spread across the high ground about 18 miles inland in the region of the Mitla Pass. The significance of this disposition of force was immediately apparent to the Egyptians, who counter-attacked in the direction of Bir Gifgafa and called in their remaining tactical air force for support.

Egyptian communications were in a bad way, and field commanders found themselves taking instructions through Radio Cairo. There were reports that the Arab alliance was despatching squadrons of aircraft. And Algeria was said to have 36 MIGs already in the area. By now it was evident to senior Egyptian officers in Sinai that no reliance could be placed upon the promises of aid. They had heard Radio Cairo's versions of campaigns in which they took part, and confidence in this official voice was destroyed. They were fighting now to save what they could of men and arms while the trap across the Mitla Pass swung shut.

ARABS STRIKE BACK reported newspapers in the West as the Egyptians rallied. But this was not a swing of the pendulum in some dingdong battle. Dozens of Russian-built tanks were being knocked out, and the response was only that of a desperate enemy who had little choice except to fight.

Matra missiles, guided by heat-seeking nosecones, slid from under the wings of Israeli Mirage–3 Cs, dropping in long flat dives across the dunes. One Israeli regiment of light tanks, slugging it out with sixty T–55s, was rocked by the explosion of its own mortar shells at a critical stage in one clash, and casualties were heavy.

The Mitla Pass became the scene of the war's last heavy encounter between opposing armor. The Pass is a narrow defile through which there is little room for tanks, but it happens to be one of the few breaks in the western ridge allowing passage to a modern desert army.

Any military expert would have given a great deal to be on the scene, and it was one of this war's many ironies that a classic battle of this nature was to move so swiftly that nobody

77

was able immediately to record it all. The Israeli armed forces make extensive use of combat correspondents and these enterprising young men and women (including General Dayan's daughter) were well aware of the need to keep up with assault units scenting victory. But army reporters were also trained for combat, and many were engulfed in fighting and thus lost sight of the general picture.

To shed a little more light, General Tal gave some details later: "Abraham Yoffe timed his push toward Bir Hasana with our penetration of the Egyptian lines in the direction of Bir Gifgafa, our two groups protecting each other's flanks . . . We destroyed an Egyptian mechanized brigade during our deployment. Additional Egyptian forces, mainly T–55 tanks, were brought up from the Canal Zone . . . It took us six hours to cover five kilometers in the subsequent move toward the Canal, with the enemy attempting to delay us with a force of one hundred tanks. We killed forty tanks and it was here the enemy was broken. This battle along a very narrow axis was conducted by sniping methods because sand dunes hemmed us in. Only three tanks led all the time. The gunners were firing up to ranges of 3,000 meters, and very accurately. The Egyptians were positioned to see us first and were always the first to fire, and for three hours there was bitter fighting between their planes and our land forces. Then our planes intervened."

The final stage came when Tal's column joined up with Yoffe again along the Canal. Missiles from the Russian SA–2 sites were then fired, but they caused limited damage. By now the Egyptians were firing across the Canal—both missiles and shells, and their aircraft made short bombing attacks. According to General Tal: "This action took place after the ceasefire. I ordered our artillery to return two shells for every shell fired at us. I believe the Egyptians learned for the first time what our border settlements near the Gaza Strip and near Syria had undergone. . . ."

A very different fight had been conducted by a girl and five boys in sandals and bluejeans from the Yad Nordecai kibbutz (named after a Warsaw Ghetto hero of the uprising against the Nazis). This kibbutz, near the Gaza Strip, had suffered 28 dead in the past ten years of terrorism by the Palestine Liberation Army. The girl and her companions streaked along a ditch and took up positions near a beleagured section of the Palestinian snipers. There they exchanged fire for the rest of the

78

day, the girl explaining that it was a pleasant change to feel free to hit back.

Meanwhile, Syria was also to see some old scores settled—on a bigger scale, but with the same insouciance. Anyone inclined to share the Old Testament belief in an eye-for-an-eye (which is, of course, what the Hebrew Bible teaches) could now appreciate Israeli emotions. Jewish soldiers give an outsider the impression of being much too intelligent and mature to indulge in histrionics. They fight gallantly, but they don't make a production of it. They must be the most undramatic of men ever to go into battle, which they do with the same matter-of-fact attitude of other craftsmen. They turned to the problem of Syria with a kind of cool contempt.

The Syrians were already running to board the ceasefire bandwagon. They had contributed most to the agony of the past few days, by their deliberate efforts to goad Nasser into belligerency; and their cowardly terrorist raids on Israeli border settlements were now to be repaid.

One of their victims for the past 19 years had been the kibbutz of Tel Katzir, or Harvest Hill, at the southeast tip of the Sea of Galilee in the Jordan valley. For the first three days and nights of the startling week of June 5, its 35 children had spent much of the time in deep shelters, while Syrian guns plastered its ten thousand verdant acres. The children and mothers sheltered while the men, mostly *sabras* in their mid-twenties, donned uniforms and went to war. The habits of the past years under fire meant that nobody panicked, and the kibbutz cows still got milked twice a day. The bunkers were supplied with small cribs for infants, and there were first-aid kits on shelves and boxes of crackers tasting like matzoh. On Monday the shelling destroyed all power. At night the children sat around candles and told stories, while neighbors from another kibbutz brought fresh water and food. By Thursday about three-quarters of the buildings had been destroyed, or badly damaged, and young trees of banana and palm were broken. About 300 Syrian shells had inflicted enough damage for the kibbutz leaders to reckon upon losing the value of a year's communal earnings—about $300,000.

Tel Katzir had made its little valley a green and pleasant oasis, and perhaps this increased Syrian resentment. Where grapes and eucalyptus grew among the watered fields of the kibbutz, the Syrians had only eroded land and scarred and

79

tawny slopes to show—and the menacing mouths of the big 105-mm howitzers dug into the sides of a mountain.

For the settlers of Tel Katzir the events of late pre-war days had been distressing. Yet open and violent war had come as a real relief. There seemed no way to bridge the gulf of bitterness which seemed to come from the Arabs, from humiliation as much as anything. Further along the shores of Galilee, for instance, was the 75-mile open ditch where the Syrians had tried to divert the headwaters of the Jordan, to deny water to the new nation where water was the greatest problem of all.

High above Galilee, in its resentful posture, the ramshackle Syrian army had been sitting since Monday, content to step up the shelling on the helpless kibbutzim. Out of Tel Katzir and other settlements went the young men, including Lieutenant Abraham Yadin who commented wryly—when someone asked him if reservists could really tackle Arab regulars: "I'm a soldier, we all are here—except we get eleven months' leave each year." For 72 hours the war with Syria was left for men like Yadin to handle. And then at noon on Friday the people of Israel launched a savage attack that smeared the land of Syria with blood and thundering destruction.

A PICTURE HISTORY OF THE ISRAELI-ARAB WAR

JUNE 1967

". . . from serious danger to successful resistance."
—*Abba Eban*
to the U.N. Security Council

THE ARAB
MOBILIZATION

"ALLAHU AKBAR!" With the
ancient Islamic rallying cry, Arab
mobs surged through the streets
of Cairo in early June. The United
Nations Emergency Force had, at the
demand of President Nasser, left
the Gaza Strip. Egyptian forces
returned to Sharm el Sheikh, and
Nasser, in an address to his armies,
declared: "Under no circumstances
will we allow the Israeli flag to pass
through the Aqaba Gulf. The Jews
threatened war. We tell them:
you are welcome, we are ready for
war ..."

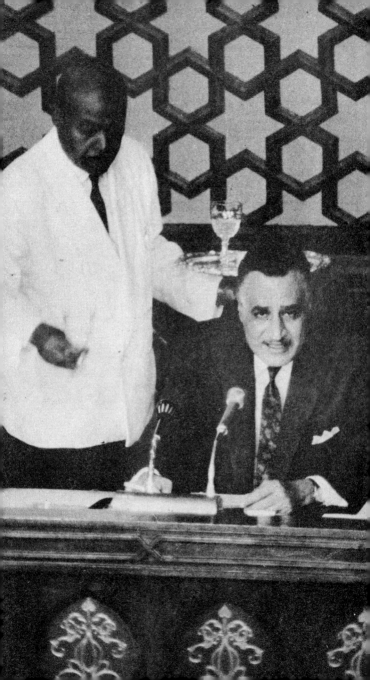

THE ISRAELI MOBILIZATION

The Gulf of Aqaba, the waterway through which Israel had received roughly 90 per cent of her vital oil supplies, was closed to Israeli shipping. Arab military alliances now threatened every border. Jordan had only to advance 20 miles to cut Israel in two. In an inflammatory speech, Nasser promised the total destruction of Israel. The menacing Arab mobilization provoked bitter memories for most Israelis. One soldier summed up the feelings of many people when he said: "I AM THE LAST SURVIVING MEMBER OF MY FAMILY FROM BUCHENWALD. THIS TIME, I HAVE A GUN TO FIGHT BACK, A COUNTRY AND A CAUSE TO SERVE!"

5 JUNE 1967

"We are a small people
but a brave one, seeking peace
but ready to fight for
its life and its country. . . .
Soldiers of Israel's Defense
Forces, in you today we
repose our hopes. . . ."

—*Israeli Defense Minister,
General Moshe Dayan,
Address to the Troops,
Jerusalem, 5 June.*

BATTLE BEGINS...

"Our people have been
waiting 20 years for this
battle. Now they will
teach Israel the lesson
of death! The Arab
armies have a
rendezvous in Israel!"
—*Radio Cairo, 5 June.*

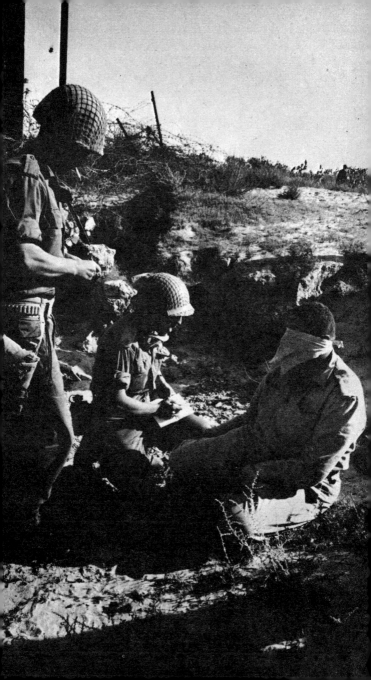

... And Moses went up to God, and the Lord called him out of the mountain, saying, "Thus you shall ... tell the people of Israel: YOU HAVE SEEN WHAT I DID TO THE EGYPTIANS, AND HOW I BORE YOU ON EAGLES' WINGS ..."

Exodus: Chapter 19

VICTORY

The battle that had begun against all odds was won. The vastly outnumbered Israelis emerged victorious after six days of fighting. People had begun to call it "The Miracle War."

The campaign had taken place during the month of *Sivan*. This, according to the Hebrew calendar, was the same month when, in ancient times, the Israelites left Egypt to wander in the wilderness of Sinai. Now, more than 3,000 years after the Exodus, they had returned— and God's message seemed to echo through the centuries. . . .

CHAPTER NINE

The tanks struck due east from the northernmost tip of Israel. The silver horn of a new moon hung above the hazy blue horizon, and the snows gleamed in the noonday sun touching the peaks of Mount Hermon. This was not tank country, but the 50-ton Centurions lurched ahead regardless, followed by columns of motorized mortars, self-propelled 105-mm Howitzers and armored infantry, and preceded by the shattering roar of Air Brigadier Hod's arrow-shaped jets.

This was a direct assault on the tough heart of the Syrian armed services which had kept in power the regime in Damascus. The crump of cannonfire was lost in the thunder of tank tracks and the boom of Mystère-4s, and farming bull-dozers which had been hastily mobilized from the border settlements moved with improvised anti-mine flails to clear a path through the frontier slope. Israeli commanders in the Tel Aviv war room listened with something more than grim satisfaction to the alarmed flurry of two-day radio conversations which their monitors were picking up from Syrian transmitters. Heavy Russian voices were heard instructing Arab tank-men on how to scramble out of the T–55s sunk like gun emplacements just inside the Syrian border.

The fury of the Israeli attack followed the claim that Syria had broken the ceasefire. In Damascus the Syrian President, Nureddin el-Atassi, cried: "We should turn the world into a hell in the face of the aggressors."

Retribution came to Syria by the most narrow of margins. Hours earlier, President Nasser had thrown in the sponge and Egypt had accepted the UN ceasefire order. It had happened on the previous afternoon in the UN where U. S. Ambassador

Arthur Goldberg was reading out another of the many proposals for restoring peace. His prospects of success seemed as dismal as ever. Then Mohammed Awad El Kony, the Egyptian Ambassador, had slipped quietly from his seat and handed U Thant a note. It was more than El Kony could do to read it himself, for it announced Cairo's final coming to terms with reality. The Secretary-General read it with no betrayal of emotion while the stricken Arab delegates buried their heads in their hands, the Americans and British shook heads in astonishment, and the Russians remained impassive.

Dr. Fedorenko was next to speak. His Russian face as impassive as ever, he denounced Israel for trampling on the soil of a foreign land "in American boots." To watch him, one would never suppose that Soviet Russia had just escaped some unfortunate consequences of meddling in the power politics of the Middle East. She had dropped Egypt and Syria by joining the ceasefire appeal after Israel had demolished or captured Russian military equipment valued at $1,500,000,-000, and from then onward it would be impossible for anyone to take Dr. Fedorenko's routine philippics at face value. He had huffed and puffed in the Arab cause, but it was clear that Moscow had no wish to be dragged into the conflict.

If this entered into the calculations of the Israeli government, nothing was said. It must have been apparent, however, that now was the time to knock Syria out of the ring. The reason given: Syria broke the ceasefire by shelling 16 settlements along the 48-mile border. Nobody by then was prepared to argue.

At Tel Katzir the mothers and children had come out of the shelters shortly after lunch to watch the Israeli jets skim across Galilee to pump shells into the fortified Syrian positions on the high ground of Golan. Nearby, the smoke hung lazily over wheatfields fired earlier by the Arab guns. A man on a bicycle rode up with a refrigerated box of Israeli ice cream, glancing apologetically at the armless sleeve of his shirt. "It's difficult to be like this, not able to fire a gun," he said.

The move into Syria fell short of Damascus for political reasons. Once again the Israeli forces displayed a sharp ear for world opinion and a sensible awareness of their own limited purpose. This was no conquering army, bent on territorial expansion. Already inside Israel there were warnings against victory parades and the lionizing of generals. Satisfaction at the outcome of a dangerous gamble there was; and soldiers thumbing rides home from the other fronts were already aware of the close shave with disaster. The tally of Russian military equipment in Egypt and Syria made it frighteningly clear that Israel had been close to extermination.

Some of this feeling emerged in a bitter speech by Premier Levi Eshkol in Tel Aviv. President Johnson had "promised great things," he said. Yet in the end Israel stood virtually alone against the Arab world.

"We were first asked to wait two days," said the Premier. "Then we sent Abba Eban to the United States and were asked to wait a further fortnight. . . . They told us that 40 to 50 maritime powers would sign a guarantee for free passage through the Tiran Strait. We examined the situation and found it came down to a dozen and finally to only two countries and then perhaps to only one—Israel."

By then Gamal Abdel Nasser had announced in Cairo his resignation as President of the United Arab Republic. He was to later "yield" to the "people's will" to remain in office.

All these were larger matters which the settlers at Tel Katzir would doubtless digest in time. For the moment they were busy welcoming home Abraham Yadin and other colonist-soldiers. Yadin told a visitor: "We must keep the Syrian heights even if the Russians wheel their biggest guns into the UN."

It seemed unlikely that any of the kibbutzim would settle for less than a buffer zone along the border. Past attempts to win Syrian cooperation in the development of the Jordan river had failed. And the headwaters were essential to any further growth of the cultivated lands extending out of the rich Huleh Valley.

A narrow rectangle of Israel between the Lebanese border and the Sea of Galilee contained the valley of settlements. It had been a part of Palestine under British mandate, and after the 1948 conflict, Syrian troops were left in possession of the southeast corner. An armistice agreement settled that Syria would withdraw and the area become demilitarized, without specifying who should control the zone. Israel insisted the territory was hers and tried to move in farmers. Syria first stopped the establishment of settlements and then embarked on it prolonged shelling of those that were finally sited in the valley. About 15,000 acres of new land were opened for cultivation by an Israeli project that drained Lake Huleh and increased the flow of Jordan water into the Sea of Galilee (known in Israel as Lake Tiberias). A plan to share the waters between Lebanon, Syria, Jordan and Israel was prepared by a special U. S. envoy, but only Israel pursued it—the Arabs refusing to participate on the grounds that it would in effect confirm Israel's right to the valley.

Israel's development schemes were ambitious, and her achievements in the first years of nationhood were such that it seemed entirely possible she would literally make the desert bloom. As if the stark landscape of the Bible and the sharp clarity of light were conducive to miracles, and visions more vividly experienced in the hot desert air, young Israelis undertook tasks that would benefit communities yet unborn. They did this in regions of hot discomfort, believing that with the odds already so heavy against her, Israel must be indeed under some special inspiration—whether divine or prophetic.

So they went ahead, unwilling to waste time. Two years ago Israel began to pump water from the Sea of Galilee into a canal and tunnel system 130 miles into the Negev. Water from the Jordan too was to have dropped over turbines to generate power before emptying into the Negev, but the Syrian guns and attempts at diversion made this impracticable.

Now the prospect opened of an Israeli-controlled border zone, 12 miles deep, with heights to block any Syrian gunners. Any democratic government in Israel was bound to heed the popular desire to end the situation whereby a neighbor could interfere in peaceful progress. For the fact remained that Israel must continue to face its problems alone; and the biggest was to restore fertility to the soil, to irrigate half the land in order to achieve self-sufficiency. The day the tanks crossed the border with the Star-of-David pennants flying was the day the settlers felt committed to preventing any further repetition of the imbecility of recent years—an idiocy dramatized when their infantry stormed the Syrian heights and descended into the gun-nests. The neglected khaki hills were tunnelled to a depth of 70 feet in order to accommodate the howitzers, and it was seen that Arabs had invested a greater energy and time in seeking to destroy Harvest Hill than they were prepared to put into making the land green. No doubt it was none of the settlers' business if the Syrian landscape remained arid, but they felt entitled, after all these years under shellfire, to hold an opinion. It was, very simply, that the Syrians deserved no sympathy.

They got very little from the Israeli troops. Joseph Grigg,

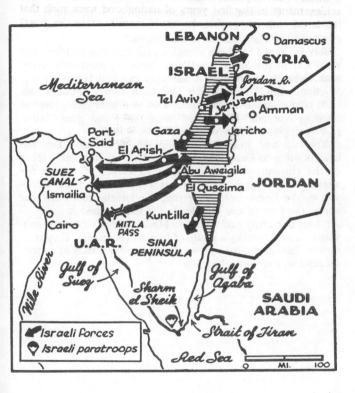

Israeli forces
Israeli paratroops

a correspondent for UPI, reported: "Syria was saved by the bell. Only a ceasefire saved it." And so, 20 kilometers from Damascus, the invaders stopped.

Correspondents, looking up at the Syrian heights shortly afterward, were astonished they had been taken at all. "Tier upon tier of trenches and gun emplacements," said a TV producer, Bill Cunningham, "all commanding the plateau below. 'How the hell did anyone get up there?' I asked. And this guy just says, 'They ran away,' and laughs."

Russian tanks had been abandoned so fast that ignition keys were still in the locks. Israeli mechanics jumped onto every usable vehicle the minute it was captured and began repairs, or cannibalized those which had been totally immobilized.

A young Israeli major said, "Did you hear about Nasser phoning Kosygin? He wanted more tanks and guns. 'Sure,' said Kosygin. 'What type does Dayan want?'"

The rich haul in captured equipment would have kept the Israelis going to Damascus. The so-called "steamroller" tactics of the close-support jets put down a carpet of intense fire ahead of the advancing columns. It seemed to Patrick O'Donovan of the *London Observer* that the Israelis could advance across the face of the Middle East if they wished it.

"Join our army and tour the Med," said a sign on a converted bus manned by a group of foreign volunteers. They were mostly Canadians, led by two doctors and a bunch of nurses, on their way to Bethlehem.

Part III: Survival

CHAPTER TEN

"The Lord came from Sinai," said Moses. Deuteronomy 33:2.

The greatest tank battle in history had taken place in the bare drift sands of the Sinai Peninsula, which projected into the Red Sea and divided it into the Gulf of Aqaba in the east and the Gulf of Suez in the west. Along its Mediterranean coast for thousands of years ran the great caravan trail linking Egypt with southwest Asia. This barren landscape, like lower Egypt, began to lose its fertility centuries ago because of camels which destroyed the green areas and the need for firewood at the ancient quarantine camp for Muslim pilgrims at Tor. The thickets of tamarisk and the clumps of acacia slowly vanished and left the bare bones of the mountain massif at the southern point of the triangle and its denuded valleys.

Here were strangely hollowed cliffs of granite and porphyry; the Mountain of the Law where God was said to have revealed himself to Moses and delivered the tables of the Law; and the beginning of the highlands on which Scripture (Genesis 2:10–14) located the earthly paradise.

Below was tank country with sandy stretches descending to the Mediterranean and an almost waterless tableland divided by the biblical River of Egypt, Wadi el-Arish. And here seven divisions of Egyptian infantry, of which two were armored, were smashed by three Israeli armored divisions supported by Air Brigadier Hod's hammering jets. Eighty thousand of the enemy and 900 of their tanks were scattered and destroyed in a titanic struggle that overshadowed the famous Battle of El Alemein.

Most of the fighting took place north of Mount Sinai but always in its shadow, either in spirit or in fact. Few of the

Israeli generals, least of all Moshe Dayan, escaped a sense of its brooding presence.

Five hundred years earlier, Felix Faber had written:

Mount Sinai seems to reach the heavens and on one of its summits God has already twice appeared, and on the other, angels in a wonderful manner laid down the body of St. Katherine the Virgin. Before Moses and Katherine both summits were unvisited by man . . . for it was the general belief that on the summit dwelt the mighty God whom no one that wished to remain alive could look upon.

Hovering above the smoking battlefields in early summer of 1967 it was possible to feel a similar sense of awe. Across this same harsh territory the ancient armies had been locked in battle too. "But do you realize how small those wars really were?" asked a special forces colonel. "In biblical times a death roll of a hundred was a disaster. War seemed more terrible then. Now?" He shrugged and stared down at the buff-colored tanks tilting like sand-beetles into the dunes below, the bodies of their dead crews still hanging from the blasted turrets. "Now," said the colonel, "you can watch the image of war on a screen, and it doesn't seem real any more. The mind gets blunted and it doesn't much matter if it's a hundred or a hundred thousand."

It mattered a great deal to Israel though. The losses were described as 679 killed, up to and including Sunday, June 11. One suddenly realized the importance of human life to a small country struggling to make a go of things, nursing its human resources. That's why there were no victory parades, no dancing in the streets, none of the swaggering bouts of drunken laughter, no tickertape processions. The losses were light when weighed against the near-destruction of a nation of nearly 2,500,000, and yet 679 fighting men and women were just 679 too many. The Arab casualty figures caused distress too. They totaled more than 35,000 dead, and of these 20,000 Egyptians had been killed.

The Israelis came back looking sober: the paratrooper who had lumbered around the dance floor in his baggy desert trousers only the week before at Mandy's, and now quietly reported that "Tony" was unfortunately one of the 679; the earnest girl student of comparative religion, linking arms with her father as they both met on a street corner outside their

Haifa home, the man back from Gaza and his daughter safely returned from the Negev; an airline hostess, Zippora Golan, taken off an incoming El Al flight to drive a bus. There were not many foreigners to witness their sombre reunions, for all the tourists had fled in the preceding weeks of crisis, but every professional observer—the correspondents and diplomats and cameramen—seemed to agree that no nation was ever less ready to celebrate. They flocked to the beaches, of course, and lay under the glorious Mediterranean sun; and friends called to each other, "So sorry about . . . ," naming a cousin or a son or a parent. The Star of David flew here and there and the chambermaids flocked back to the Hilton and the Sheraton and the Dan and chattered briefly about where they had been—to Beersheba or Haifa, relieving men for the front. And then fell silent.

There was a moment on the night of Monday, June 12 when the ferocity of the desert burst into a crowded Tel Aviv hall. A week had gone by, a week when the world had shifted on its axis. In an army conference room, through the rear doors that burst open as if commandos were kicking their way in, four Israeli generals appeared.

They were fresh from Sinai and they moved each one like a cat alone, heel and toe. They were Ariel "Arik" Sharon, the paratrooper; "Shaike" Gavish, who commanded the Sinai forces; Abraham Yoffe, the conservationist, who led the reservists; and Israel Tal of the Armored Corps.

They unrolled maps and described the Sinai operations which had moved so swiftly that few observers had caught up with the spearhead forces. One who did was John Wallace of the *London Daily Telegraph* who had appeared outside his hotel in a business suit, complete with rolled umbrella, on the first morning and instructed his taxi driver: "Take me to the Gaza Strip."

Abraham laughed when he heard the story and said that was how a lot of his own men got to their units "three weeks ago," which was when the frontline troops had slipped quietly into their positions. He was the biggest of the generals, "built like a tank," he said in a booming cockney voice. He stuck his thumbs into his belt, and the revolver on his hip swung back as he said, "I got the job of penetrating the Egyptian lines because of my weight, I suppose." His division had struck the Canal inside four days and knocked out 157

89

tanks. "I protect nature in civilian life," he said, studying the Sinai map. "This time I protected my country." It might have sounded theatrical from anyone less spontaneous.

Israel, the Galilean, was half Abraham's size. He wiped the back of his hand across his dusty face and grinned at a girl corporal. "Look," he said, "our army is an army of boys under National Service—oh, and some girls too . . ." He ducked his head at the corporal. "A lot of the tank crews are reservists. Now operating a modern tank is very complicated and the Egyptians put regular soldiers with many years' experience in their tanks. Our boys get very short periods of National Service to learn the armorers' trade and reach a standard better than the enemy's. So we didn't build up our armor along conventional lines, but we tried to find new and very unconventional methods of operating a tank force and fighting with it. The secret element, the method which proved itself—well, we always taught our fighters to go deep, penetrate right behind enemy lines and never mind your unprotected flanks, but upset the enemy's equilibrium and attack him from behind and inside. You can teach this in lectures but you can't do it without superior tankmen. . . .

"We had old tanks, tanks from the Second World War. The enemy, both in Egypt and Syria, had the most modern tanks from the Russians, sometimes before they went into Soviet service. We tried to improve our tanks, the old tanks, by improvisation—by getting better gear, better guns. But in any case we couldn't improve our tanks so they compare or compete with the most modern type the enemy has. Even the tanks sold us during the last few years are not the most modern. They're tanks which became obsolete in Western armies."

He ducked and weaved his head, prodding the other generals. He'd mounted 105-mm guns on the Centurions, which weren't built for that weight of fire, and he'd stripped down some of the armor. He'd goosed the old Shermans to get another fraction of speed out of them, and he'd invented a kind of "porcupine" attack—the unit rolled into the enemy camp and then discharged its "quills." But he wasn't saying precisely how all this was done. He'd studied the Soviet army textbook defenses for Arab positions, and he'd worked out the weak spots. He was just a quick-witted farm boy from Galilee who'd fought in the Jewish Brigade in Italy and knew his way around, and he knew how to parry questions that probed too deep.

Ariel was, like the others, a product first of Haganah, the Jewish underground defense movement. His manner was more scholarly though, befitting a student of Mideast history. He knew the histories of the Egyptian kings in Sinai and he had poked around the mountain and dug up relics. When he said about a thousand tanks clashed for a day and night near the Mitla Pass, you knew he would have precise figures, because he was that kind of man. The last time he had broken through to the Pass, 11 years before against the same enemy, he had run ahead of himself. General Dayan had commented later: "The backbone of an army's strength is the urge and readiness to push ahead. . . . If no such spirit permeated the ranks, it's likely fewer mistakes would be made, but Sinai would not be won."

This time Ariel had permission to go, and at the Pass he tried to radio General Dayan, "but like the last time, I didn't make the connection." He added, almost like an afterthought, "It took us three-and-a-half days to break through."

Shaike, a balding general with steady blue eyes, summarized the Sinai actions, which had been so different from the 1956 methods. The whole peninsula had been under his command, and it was an awesome thought. He, too, was acutely aware of history.

We found 38 struck down, wrote an eyewitness of the massacre of the Forty Martyrs of Sinai, the monk Ammonius of Canopus in 373. *Their limbs were cut off, heads severed. The King of the Saracens had been killed and these were blamed.*

"Yes, a violent territory," agreed the man who commanded it. And he went on to describe how he ordered the tanks to smash the Egyptian forces once and for all.

The hero, inevitably, was General Dayan. In the cautious postwar mood, however, any tendency to lionize him was discouraged and one of his younger officers said, quite bluntly, "He's a great tactician but he'd make the wrong kind of leader." He was a forthright man who came close to sounding as if the war had been launched by Israel as a preventive campaign. Many understood that preventive war was a mere term: Dayan had lashed out like a fighter who sees the telltale flicker in his opponent's eye.

So the attitude of his men was ambivalent: proud on the one hand, but also aware of his shortcomings as a democratic figure. There was a strong wave of disillusionment with politicians who had been so much slower than Dayan to face the need for action. The traditional hostility between decisive men and intellectuals, always ready to hear the other side, deepened. "All the same," said Menachem Begin, the rabbi-turned-guerilla, "it's significant this country has *not* feted Dayan like a conquering hero. There's too strong a distrust of military minds."

Begin believed that Dayan's group of top officers had brought off a brilliant victory in the very teeth of disaster, and so did the military planners who knew how very close the Russian-backed Arabs had been to success. They also knew of the meeting between Dayan and David Ben-Gurion, when the old man—looking more like a prophet than ever—had warned the general against a military adventure that might again leave Israel open to suspicion of suffering from a nervous twitch. The old arguments started up again: how long *could* a potential victim of aggression wait for trouble to start, when the first blow meant so much? The one consistent figure in all this was Dayan himself, whose views had not changed since he had written in his diary after the first Sinai campaign: "All the way up the Gulf of Elath I could not tear my eyes from the window. We flew low, and the reefs of coral skirting the coast below the limpid surface of the shallow water were clearly visible. . . . In New York at the UN heavy pressure is being exerted against us. They demand our withdrawal, without guaranteeing freedom of navigation for our ships in the Red Sea, and without ensuring that Sinai will not again become a base for Egyptian aggression. . . . What disturbs me is not the end of the fighting but my apprehension about our capacity to hold our own in the political campaign which now begins. . . ."

Flying over the same route, I wondered if Israel was doomed to fight these campaigns at regular intervals, as some of her leaders feared, unless some other understanding could be reached with the Arabs. Dayan had told me, when I put the question: "Times change."

The only visible change now was the even greater wreckage of war. Tanks and half-tracks, howitzers and jeeps covered the sands in incredible confusion.

Hundreds of 120-mm all purpose Russian guns, some with

cloth protectors still wrapped over their muzzles, were assembled as if on parade. Packing cases for Soviet-built rockets lay scattered like toys. Long trails of discarded clothing wriggled back toward the distant Nile, boots and helmets and webbing cast aside by fleeing Egyptians and looking like the debris that follows the wake of a ship.

The Mitla Pass was choked with burned and overturned tanks. Clearly there had never been a struggle like this one. The leading Egyptian tanks, monsters including the lumbering Stalin fortresses, had been stopped in their tracks by air assault. Those behind had been unable to overtake before pursuing Israeli armor began to drop shells into the confusion from ranges up to 3,000 meters. Some damaged Egyptian tanks had obviously attempted to cut around those ahead, and slowly the dreadful pileup began as these became bogged in sand. Like red ants racing over the obstacles ahead, the Egyptian tanks and trucks, half-tracks and howitzers, and all the strange equipment men take to war, all this mobile armor had spread up the pass until it choked to a stop. Then the final carnage began and the results were as if a child had dropped boxes of toy soldiers and hundreds of toy metal trucks and tanks into a pool of black treacle.

"Poor devils," said an Israeli regimental commander, nodding down at the Egyptian bodies bursting in the sun. "They were fighting in a strange desert with nothing but a dictator's words to inspire them. They kicked off their boots in order to run better because these people are too poor to wear boots in normal times. They were given golden fountain pens and they couldn't even write."

CHAPTER ELEVEN

We were Pharaoh's bondmen in Egypt and the Lord
brought us out of Egypt with a mighty hand; and the
Lord shewed signs and wonders, great and sore, upon
Egypt, upon Pharaoh, and upon all his household, before our eyes; and He brought us out from thence, that
He might bring us in, to give us the land which He
sware unto our fathers.

—Deuteronomy 26:5–9

The strange things that happen to men in war took place
so swiftly in Sinai that many of the stories only began to be
told in the days after the war ended, as soldiers slowly adjusted
to the fact there *had* been a war and the week of it was no
dream. Perhaps this is how legends are created. Around
Mount Sinai the fantastic colors of the heights and the great
tawny plains vibrating in temperatures of 113 degrees would
certainly aid the imagination. Yet there was no doubt about
the reality of certain events; and many of those who saw them
were in normal times farmers and kibbutzim who were well
accustomed to see visions become facts and miracles enter into
everyday life.

A girl corporal with no claim to any special awareness of
religion said she was riding in a half-track with the regimental
commander of an armor unit when she saw immediately in
their path a tremendous fire leap up. The commander could
see nothing and the girl, thinking his sand goggles were covered in dust, yelled to him to swerve aside. He, convinced of
danger because he knew the girl well enough, but still unable
to see anything, swung away into another opening that appeared between the dunes, and the rest of the column followed. Only a jeep, flying along almost parallel with the
leading half-track and blinded by swirling sand, motored on.
The girl turned to where the fire should be, moments after
the column changed direction, and to her consternation saw

nothing. Then an explosion shook the area and the straying jeep disappeared. It had driven straight into an Egyptian minefield.

There was documentary and visual proof of the extraordinary passage of the first merchant ship to transit the Strait of Tiran. It was a Soviet ship sailing to Aqaba in Jordan, and the Russian captain, not knowing who was in possession of the commanding point at Sharm el Sheikh, asked permission to proceed. He was given it by Lieutenant-Commander David Balva, whose navy torpedo boats had beaten the paratroopers to the Egyptian positions.

"For us," Ben-Gurion had said about the 1956 campaign, "the main purpose of the Sinai campaign was to safeguard our southern sea route." He had set in motion a series of contingency plans so that if another clash should occur, Israel could take over the triangle with clockwork precision. These included the use of Israeli frogmen; and another of the strange stories that emerged, never to be officially confirmed, was that one team of underwater demolition experts chanced upon Egyptian warships when they were aboard one of their own vessels on a routine reconnaissance.

Some secrecy about the Sinai operations was inevitable because Israel had made plain in the past its concern for the Negev Desert. The settlement of this "empty half" had taken first place in Ben-Gurion's order of priorities for developing Israel because "if the state does not put an end to the desert, the desert will put an end to the state. We shall become a city-state like Carthage," he said. Then, too, the colonization of the Negev would make Israel more securely a part of the Asian continent, which Ben-Gurion considered to be Israel's environment, "no matter how much our own way of life happens to be modeled on that of Europe."

This powerful sense of forcing new life out of the barren desert and of making this harsh land part of its natural surroundings was, of course, where Ben-Gurion's policies had seemed wrong to some immigrants from the West—especially North America, where the pioneer spirit was not quite up to conditions that must have seemed impossible. For instance Ruth Halliday in her study of the Negev, *The Skills to Make the Desert Bloom* (Anglo-Israel Association, 1966), described a settlement near Sodom where "the summer temperature rises to 46–50 degrees centigrade [115–122 F.], there is no fresh drinking water, the hot desert winds blow all day and night, and there is nothing to relieve the monotony of the scene . . . No one believed it could be possible to grow anything in such a spot or even to survive there and so no funds were forthcoming to aid the venture . . . They went ahead . . . Today there are large areas of forage grass grown to feed the cattle . . . fields of tomato, onions, eggplants and melons, large fishponds . . ."

Much will be written, no doubt, about divisions of opinion among Israel's leaders concerning "hard" and "soft" policies toward the Arab threat. I would say these divisions are healthy democratic ones, and if Moshe Dayan, appointed Minister of Defense at the last minute, seemed to have introduced the influence of "hawks" this did not necessarily mean the "doves" were defeated.

It did mean a difference in feelings toward Sinai, toward the fierce Ben-Gurion view of making deserts bloom, and a softer attitude that it wasn't worth risking periodic wars for the sake of empty desert.

"It's great to be Prime Minister in a country of a million presidents," said Levi Eshkol with his typical Yiddish humor.

He was discussing the dissensions that preceded war. An aide said Israel was like a family of nomads surrounded by hungry wolves, arguing if they should shoot the wolves or throw them food. "That's the way a democratic society is destroyed," he said. "Too many intellectuals and they're all arguing while the enemy attacks."

But Premier Eshkol disagreed. He considered that a free society should in the end defeat a dictatorship. He suggested Israel could well afford to achieve consensus before deciding how to handle Nasser's latest challenge. He was right, as it turned out.

The personalities and backgrounds of those who guided Israel are instructive. The outcome of their arguments is encouraging in an age when pessimists wonder if intellectual freedom can survive when bullies are armed with weapons so swift that the first blow is usually fatal.

Eshkol himself grew up with Israel. He landed at Jaffa from a tramp steamer as a 17-year-old Ukrainian immigrant in 1914 and helped to establish a kibbutz in a malarial swamp. He was a practical socialist and helped to build the labor organization Histadrut, which today runs nearly half the economy. He knows the Nazi mind extremely well and has always been highly informed on its influence in Cairo. He

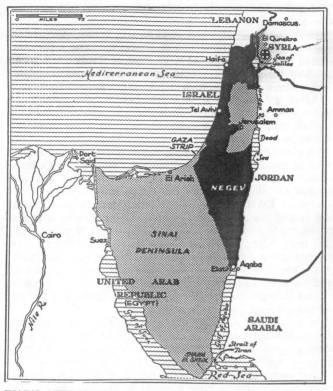

WAR'S AFTERMATH: Israel said war in the Middle East had wiped out past armistice pacts and indicated borders (dark shading) would have to change. Area overrun by her forces is in light shading. Cease-fire in the Syrian area (cross) was accepted.

spent three years in Berlin helping to get Jews out of Hitler's Germany, and to obtain arms for the underground Jewish army at home. He founded the postwar arms industry that is slowly giving Israel a degree of independence from foreign suppliers of weapons. He shaped the exciting years from 1952 to 1963 when Israel's economy blossomed. He was then Finance Minister and he directed foreign capital into constructive projects and raised more money abroad by the sale of Israeli bonds.

97

An almost mystical attachment to the Negev was evident among Ben-Gurion's old friends ("disciples" is not inappropriate here). As a "retired" general, for instance, Moshe Dayan made a tour of desert units when he felt, before most people had adjusted to the likelihood of a new war, that a time for action was coming. He went to Premier Eshkol who gave permission. "I knew we could rely on the settler-soldiers" he said later. "I met the men and field commanders. There was this feeling I had that Israel would have to give up and accept whatever compromise we could get, or strike back. I wanted to look at latest defense plans and whatever information we had from the other side."

He came back from the Sinai so convinced of trouble that when it seemed he could not have the position of Defense Minister, he refused any other cabinet post and told the Premier to "mobilize me for the Negev."

Premier Eshkol had always deplored Dayan's flamboyance and feared the general would make too impetuous a prime minister. He wanted, as Defense Minister, Yigal Allon, who had once talked to Nasser when the Egyptian leader was trapped in the Faluja Pocket in 1948. Nasser had questioned Allon about the Jewish underground fight with the British, and he gave Allon the impression that in certain circumstances it might be possible for Israel to work with Nasser for the common good of the Middle East.

In the sense of a destiny fulfilled that followed the destruction of Russian weapons in the Sinai, the old squabbles were starting again. And with reason. The war ended with Israel in grave need to secure peace on more livable terms.

This meant arriving at a policy which would reflect Israel's unity and her determination never to be exposed again to the infiltration of such huge forces into an apparently empty peninsula.

Premier Eshkol's popularity was weakened by poor speaking ability (his accent is still heavily Ukrainian). He had been Ben-Gurion's trouble-shooter but they quarreled over a misconceived sabotage plot in Cairo known as the Lavon Affair. Eshkol was *heimish*, plain folk, and he disliked making dramatic appeals to the public. He lacked Ben-Gurion's theatrical wings of white hair and Dayan's eyepatch appeal.

Abba Eban, the Foreign Minister, was criticized for putting too much faith in Washington. He persuaded the cabinet to seek maritime-power support to open the Strait of Tiran.

Some thought his belief in sweet reasonableness very nearly brought defeat. Yet Eban did a great deal to convey Israel's sense of national peril when he addressed the UN. He was a former Cambridge don who fought Nasser-type Arab fanaticism while seeing a necessity to come to terms with the Arabs. "Prevention of war," he had said, "comes prior to the achievement of peace."

Yigal Allon was a former fighting general whose leftwing views conflicted with Dayan's more forthright approach. He was Minister of Labor and almost took over as Defense Minister in the hasty organization of the Government of National Emergency on the eve of war. He had said on previous occasions that it was more important for Israel to avert a war than to win one.

Mrs. Golda Meir illustrated better than any perhaps the total involvement of Israel, so that the task of picking out a national hero—easy enough for the foreign press—was difficult. Ill-health had forced her to retire from the post of Foreign Minister but she had been in the forefront of Jewish leadership for 40 years and she was right behind Eban's campaign to present to the world the true picture of the crisis. Born in Kiev 69 years ago, the daughter of a carpenter, she had gone to Milwaukee to escape Russian pogroms against Jews. She understood Washington's dilemma in the crisis but was hardheaded enough to expect little U.S. support if Dayan and the "hawks" triggered the war.

Yigael Yadin was another soldier-archeologist, but unlike Dayan he was respected among intellectuals. He was Chief of Staff in the 1948 war and since then he did more than anyone to rescue the Dead Sea scrolls and to excavate Masada.

These were some of the leaders who demonstrated Israel's diversity of talents and views. They differed, but not in common loyalty to their country. If Dayan seemed hotheaded it was well to remember he had a powerful sense of history and a passionate love of the desert and what it could mean to Israel. If Premier Eshkol seemed to be the Great Compromiser, as indeed he was called, it was wise to remember that he had been seared by the childhood experience of cowering behind barricades with his family during the anti-Jewish pogroms that followed the Russo-Japanese War and "I was unable to forget how we never thought of striking back. When I was older I wanted to know what I would do if the Jews were ever attacked like that again."

99

CHAPTER TWELVE

The forces of imperialism imagine that Abdel Nasser is their enemy. I want it to be clear to them it is the entire Arab nation and not Gamal Abdel Nasser. The forces hostile to the Arab nationalist movement always try to picture it as Abdel Nasser's empire. That is not true, for the hope for Arab unity began before Gamal Abdel Nasser. It will remain after Gamal Abdel Nasser.

—Gamal Abdel Nasser's resignation speech,
June 9, 1967

At 3:30 A.M. on May 26 the Soviet Ambassador in Cairo asked urgently to see President Nasser. Shortly thereafter he delivered a request from the Kremlin that the United Arab Republic should not be the first to open fire in the tense situation which had developed on the Israeli border. A similar request had been given to the U.A.R. ambassador in Washington only a few hours earlier. Yet Nasser ignored these warnings. Why?

There were pressures upon him that the Israeli government's Arab specialists thought ominous. In a world which was not yet adjusted to mass adoration, a world which no longer permitted the total demolition of an enemy, leaders with the peculiar appeal of Nasser, Mao Tse-tung, or other dictators, were not the norm. Arabs, like others living in the Afro-Asian world, were filled with bitterness for an unhappy past they blamed upon white imperialism. They had lost their age-old gods under the weight of new ideas. They turned to leaders gifted with eloquence and the ability to arouse deep emotions of racial pride. The Arabs adored Nasser even in defeat. His attempt to resign after five days of humiliating defeat was greeted with alarm and an immediate demand for his return.

Even if some of the demand was artificial, it illustrated the dangerous mood of millions who saw in Nasser the embodiment of all their half-crushed hopes. "Trust me!" he cried on the day his tanks wobbled back across the Canal, and trust him a great number did, for he thereupon repeated the astonishing lie which earlier excused Arab defeat. He said again that Anglo-American aircraft raided the Arab positions, in support of Israel. This is what Arabs wanted to believe to salve their pride; and it was especially unfortunate from Israel's viewpoint, because in 1956 something of the kind had really happened, against the better judgment of some Israeli strategists. They could have done, they said at the time, without Anglo-French interference.

It seemed hard to divine Nasser's intentions when he made the fateful move of concentrating his forces in the Sinai— "a natural geographic barrier," as Israel's Foreign Minister had said, "separating the main forces of the two sides."

Egypt was in poor economic shape, according to Israeli intelligence. It discovered an urgent commercial debt of $2 million which Cairo could not pay. Secret negotiations were in progress with Britain to resume diplomatic relations by July 1, and an Egyptian army dignitary had assured an informal inquirer from Ottawa that troop movements in Sinai were only of political consequence.

Yet suddenly Nasser was launched upon a series of actions which seemed to lead irreversibly to war. The violence of Nasser's language stung Philip Toynbee to write to the *London Times:* "President Nasser affirms the Arab intention is to massacre every Israeli or at least enforce the exodus of the whole Israeli population. These aims are wicked, mad, and insupportable."

The surprising pact in the week preceding war with King Hussein was another long step toward the abyss. Cairo in the past had denounced the Jordanian King as a traitor to the Arab cause. The sudden publicity given to a bellicose Peking-trained troublemaker, Ahmed Shukairy, was further evidence of Nasser's new recklessness. Shukairy led the Palestine Liberation Organization, which was the front for terrorists groomed by Communist China in politico-guerilla war.

Nasser's ferocious abuse of the Jews was now causing acute anxiety among foreign politicians who might have helped

101

him. The British socialists were up in arms. Lord Fraser drew a parallel between Nazi Germany and the declared intention of Egypt and Syria to raze Israel from the map. The French socialist leader Daniel Mayer said: "I am ashamed to be a socialist if that epithet is applied to the Russian policy of encouraging the Arab nations. I am ashamed to be a Frenchman since the official policy of my country means abandoning in the hour of peril a friend. But I am proud to be a Jew."

Of course there had been Syria's deliberate goading, and Jordan's taunts about Nasser hiding behind the UN, to make him try again to justify his claim to be the leader of Arab nationalism. Yet it was still difficult to see why he crossed the line between words and action: between making his characteristic moves in a cloud of oratory, and committing himself to the closure of the Strait of Tiran which at once inflamed Arab passions and set Israel's neighbors baying for blood.

The *baraka*, the "blessing" which gave Nasser his particular aura among Arabs, was perhaps to blame. It filled him with superconfidence. It robbed him of the criticism which is just as essential to a leader as brakes and steering are to a car. It gave him godlike wisdom in the eyes of the masses. His broad face, dark eyes, heavy brows, gleaming teeth, his oddly Charlie Chaplin mustache and crinkly hair, these became familiar from the caves of the Yemen to the hovels of Morocco as the features of a talisman.

The burden of such hero worship was more than any man could bear without losing perspective, and Nasser was not a particularly philosophic man. He decided early that Israel was an imperialist plot against the Arab world, and unfortunately he chose some sinister advisors in the period when he needed outside help and would not take it from those he regarded as former oppressors.

A stream of former Nazis had been arriving in Cairo in the 1950's and they found the political climate to their liking. They sent word to old comrades in Latin America, and soon Egypt was giving haven to men who could get no nearer to Europe without risking identification. They included Leopold Gleim, once Gestapo chief in Warsaw; SS General Oscar Dirlewanger and Willi Brenner, who organized the Mauthausen concentration camp; General Wilhelm Fahrmbacher, an artillery specialist who brought 34 ex-German army officers with him. Dr. Wilhelm Voss took charge of a missile production center and was joined by Professor Paul Goerke of Peenemünde.

Some Germans still embarrassed by their Nazi backgrounds were given Arab names, among them Dr. Johann von Leers, who had been a leading anti-Jewish propagandist. Nasser employed some in his propaganda agencies and others in the development of weapons. They served, knowingly or not, an Arab resurgence of pride which was being distorted into hate.

In other respects Nasser had won a qualified admiration from the West for his early skill in obtaining aid by playing off one power group against another. "Positive neutralism" was the tag he gave a policy that eased Britain out of the Sudan and Suez, and put him in partnership with Communist as well as imperialist states. He captured much of the limelight at the first Bandung Conference in 1955 when the "third world" of Afro-Asians began to emerge as a force. His first big display of a basic flaw was the way he nationalized the Suez Canal in a flash of rage over refusal of Western aid for the Aswan High Dam.

He seemed to sense the new opportunities awaiting any leader willing to gamble on the East-West power balance. None of the great powers wanted to risk war in a nuclear age and he exploited this, perceiving that rivalries now took the form of winning allies through aid. The aborted Anglo-French attacks in the Suez crisis won him tremendous acclaim. He had defied Western might. From then on, he was the man who restored Arab self-respect after centuries of foreign domination. His influence spread and he became in many ways the creature of the new forces abroad among Arabs. Syria threw herself into his astonished arms and the United Arab Republic was formed. His "socialist" philosophy with its similarity to disciplined National Socialism was used to cover a multitude of Arab reformist movements.

There were setbacks as he approached his fifties. He was no longer a promising young colonel but a slightly rumpled and middle-aged bombast who had to pull fresh surprises out of the hat to keep his audience. His attempts to expand Egypt's economy in every direction met with sympathy abroad, but it was evident that he was unwilling to devote much time to economic matters. The rapid growth in population was running beyond his capacity to improve conditions.

His leadership of the Afro-Asian world had long since

shown itself to be a dream. He competed with Israel in the developing countries, but again the contrast in methods was instructive. Egyptian teachers were primarily concerned with making propaganda, and technical advisors proved to lack experience, so that recipients of Egyptian aid soon recognized it as an unusually crude attempt to exert influence. Israel on the other hand ran a flexible and economic program to provide technical assistance in 62 countries, and Israeli technicians (about a thousand by 1967) were generally welcomed. Some 2,500 students came from Afro-Asian countries to study in Israel and on the whole such Israeli schemes were successful, although the element of political competitiveness was apparent in African states where Egypt was seeking influence.

The old *baraka* was getting tarnished when Nasser ran into difficulties. Syria seceded from the U.A.R. and Cairo was losing influence in the Afro-Asian organizations. In 1967 Egyptian soldiers were still making a poor showing after five years of guerilla war in Yemen, during which they were accused of using poison gas.

Above all, Nasser had set Israel up as the archenemy of Arabs and he had still done nothing about it. He must have felt frustrated, and much of the Arab world was certainly curious about his inability to neutralize this contemptibly small state.

His moves against Israel, in the light of his past, were indicative of a man who thought he could get away with international misbehavior again. And later, when he had been taught differently, the question asked in Tel Aviv was whether or not the UN must take much of the blame for encouraging leaders like Nasser to believe they could flout the normal rules. If he miscalculated, how much of his misjudgment was a result of failure at the UN to evolve an efficient and disinterested machinery for preventing any nation from overstepping the limits of provocation?

In the immediate aftermath of the war, there was no great atmosphere of celebration in Israel. For one thing the Jews are not disposed to gloat. For another, although their losses were light for the murderous battles they had won, even a single death in action seemed a terrible thing to these people, who had learned thrift in human life above all things. But in addition to all this, Israel was deeply aware of the problems ahead, and placed upon Nasser's survival an interpretation that was far from encouraging. Even if his retention of the Presidency were short-lived, the manner of it was significant.

His initial resignation aroused emotions throughout the Arab world. Broadcasters wept, crowds rioted, politicians protested, and in one capital after another the embassies of the West were attacked by angry mobs.

The Israeli triumph had been too great. Arabs turned fearfully to the father figure and heard him voice the same doubts as they. In their anguish they could not admit his fallibility, and they demanded he remain. If he plotted the whole thing by some diabolical knowledge of the Arab mind, if he knew this was the way to keep power by wearing a martyr's wreath, he caused a reaction that warned the outside world of problems to come. "The destruction of imperialism in the Arab world leaves Israel with its own strength alone," he said. "Whatever the conditions, and however long they last, the abilities of the Arabs are greater and more effective."

This pathetic assertion of Arab greatness only emphasized the all-pervading sense of Arab weakness.

One Arab leader who did not suffer from crippling, secret feelings of inferiority was Vice-President Zakariah Mohieddin, who was named by Nasser as his successor before Nasser withdrew his resignation. The Vice-President's name means "Reviver" (of Islam), and his emergence, if real, would have augured well for Israel as well as the Prophet. However, it was possible he had been named by Nasser in a further attempt to push Russia into taking a more active part in the war, because Mohieddin is significantly less anti-Western than other veterans of the original Free Officers who have held senior posts in the last 15 years.

Mohieddin is a remote man, keeping his own counsel in a land where gossip is freer than water, and a close friend of Nasser. He inherited wealth but he is acutely conscious of poverty. He gave up much of his land voluntarily but unobtrusively when agrarian reform was introduced. He is 49 and served as an infantry officer in the Palestine War.

It is said Mohieddin has in the past formed amiable relations with Israelis. He broke the power of the Moslem Brotherhood when he was Minister of the Interior in 1954, and the paradox is that he gave Egyptians a glimpse of political freedom—*after* he served as top cop in a military dictatorship. For a year (1965) he was Prime Minister and his policies put the economy into better condition than it had been for

105

a long time. Six bumbling directors of public enterprises were toppled and efficiency crept into a bureaucracy which had sheltered too many freeloaders.

Under Mohieddin restrictions were lifted on Egyptians wishing to go abroad. Then Arab nationalism became assertive again and late in 1966 the first premier to display initiative in the Nasser era was put out to grass. He once said, "We shall have to come to terms with Israel some day," and he was one of the Egyptian leaders who were regarded as "not unfriendly" in Jerusalem. Within a week of hostilities ending, feelers were being put out by the Israel government to see if Mohieddin did now exercise influence again, and might be willing to enter into direct talks.

The desire to be alone in talks with the Arabs was freely voiced on the day the leaders made their first pilgrimage to the Wailing Wall. Reports from the battle fronts said thousands of Arab soldiers were lost in the desert. Their plight dramatized the problem of refugees, regarded as fundamental to any reconciliation between Israel and her neighbors. The view in Jerusalem was that 1,500,000 refugees, added to Israel's present bedouin population, would destroy the state. An opposing argument was that of the publisher-politician Uri Avnery, who had several times suffered public anger for his defense of Arab rights. He estimated 300,000 refugees were in Gaza; 500,000 on the west bank of the Jordan; 300,-000 on the east bank; and about 280,000 between Lebanon and Syria. It was his contention that until Israel actively helped to settle the refugees, there would always be a festering Arab resentment toward his country.

One week after the war began, the *Jerusalem Post* reported that Israeli leaders wanted to discuss the issue with the Arabs "not as conquerors but as collaborators doing something for a mucked-up corner of the world." It seemed a reassuringly generous sentiment to appear on the same day as the casualty lists.

CHAPTER THIRTEEN

"The Israel defense forces dominate the Sinai Peninsula as far as the Suez Canal, the west bank of the Jordan and the Golan Heights. The passage through the Strait of Tiran to the Gulf of Aqaba is free. Jerusalem is reunited. For the first time since the establishment of the state, Jews pray at the Western Wall, the relic of our sacred Temple and our historic past, and at Rachel's Tomb. For the first time in our generation Jews can make their devotions at the Cave of Machpela in Hebron, the city of the patriarchs. The prophecy has been fulfilled. 'There is recompense for the work; the sons have returned to their borders.' "

So spoke Israel's Premier a week after the war began. But not all the sons had returned. The newspapers, which had managed to reach every corner of the country even in the height of battle, now began to publish the death notices. The *Jerusalem Post* carried many like these:

SEGEN EHUD SHANI
has fallen in battle
for the liberation of Jerusalem.
                    The family.

AIR FRANCE
share the deep sorrow of the family of
RONALD AZOULAY
who fell in action for Israel.

The Director and Staff of the Government Press Office
mourn the death of three colleagues who fell in line of duty
Ben Oyserman—Canadian Broadcasting Corporation
Paul Schutzer—*Life* Magazine
Frederick Langdon Yates, Jr.—National Broadcasting Corporation

*   *   *

Hospitals were dealing methodically with the wounded and again the figures seemed light: 2,563 injured had been counted, a fraction of the expected figure on which the General Staff based its plans for the concentration of doctors and nurses. Indeed there was now a surplus of medical men from overseas—"Every Jewish family earmarks one son for doctoring," said Dr. David Levi in Jerusalem, "and it seemed as if every other Jewish family overseas had sent a doctor here."

People began to understand in cold detail just what might have happened if the battle had gone the other way. The preparations against gas attack had been accepted calmly enough but when a mobile Russian decontamination chamber was hauled out of the Sinai along with other equipment supplied to the Egyptians the full implications began to sink in.

The decontamination chamber was boldly labeled "Made in Russia—Ministry of Health Disinfectant and Chemical Equipment Works." Army officers were careful to draw no conclusions—after all, they said, *actual* poison gas had not been found in the weaponry of the Egyptian forces in Sinai—but there were gas masks, and the alternative explanation that this was a field decontamination unit didn't seem very convincing. The unit from which the mobile chamber was taken had been in service in Yemen against royalist forces and poison gas was used there. It was recalled how reluctant the world had been to believe stories of gas in Yemen—Richard Beeston of the *London Daily Telegraph* first reported Egyptian use of it some years earlier, and despite his distinguished record as a correspondent, he was accused until 1966 of fabricating the story. Then irrefutable evidence was obtained, too late to save victims during the period when the rest of the world preferred to believe Cairo's hot denials. Suddenly, too, Israelis remembered the frantic last-minute attempt by their government to buy gas masks abroad; and the truth leaked out that highly placed intelligence sources in Cairo had warned the Israeli Chief of Staff, Major-General Yitzhak Rabin, of indications the Egyptians would use gas. In the last few days before the war began, Israel's representatives abroad made a desperate search for Second World War gas masks and located a large number in West Germany. (By contrast, two members of a CBC crew trying to join me in Tel Aviv spent a fruitless day combing London for masks. They finally located some by asking where the British army bought theirs. The answer was, a private firm of outfitters.)

The two-ton Russian missiles, which had been reported in the Sinai within 24 miles of the Israeli nuclear center near Beersheba, now made their frightening appearance among the citizens who were to have been their target. Their range was, in fact, 24 miles. Nine had been captured intact, complete with carrier cocked for action.

Until now, the presence of rockets and missiles and all the deadly paraphernalia credited to the German and Russian supporters of Nasser had seemed somehow as unreal as Nasser's propaganda itself. Now the living proof made its obscene appearance and the question was asked: Why were none fired?

The radar-controlled missile put on display was the SA-2 model used in North Vietnam. Altogether 11 SA-2 sites had been identified around Cairo and the Nile Delta, or on the Israel side of the Suez Canal, during preliminary high-level aerial reconnaissance. The first air strikes of Monday, June 5, took out two of these sites. Yet only one Israeli fighter was destroyed by missile attack, although Egyptians launched a large number between Monday and Wednesday. The failure of the missiles seemed to lie with the Egyptians, although Peking Radio immediately claimed the reason was that Russia supplied the missiles with a built-in electronic double lock so that launchings could be made only when a Russian was present.

What about the rockets? German scientists had been working for years to build liquid-fuel rockets that Egypt could manufacture. The ground-to-ground "Al Kahir" and "Al Zafir" rockets had always given operational trouble although they were great for impressing the crowds at military parades. A team of German experts under the Scientific Director of the Stuttgart Jet Propulsion Study Institute, Eugen Sänger, had been forced to abandon their work at Base 333, the Egyptian rocket establishment in the desert near Heliopolis, after the Israeli government put pressure on Bonn; but the *Sängerknaben* (Sänger's choirboys) contrived to soldier on. Their labors, more heavily disguised, bore rotten fruit. Egypt lacked the ability to manufacture propulsion fuel and the graphite-lined combustion chambers kept bursting.

News of this kind of ineptitude had filtered back to Israel and thus the rockets became merely Nasser propaganda in many minds. The shock of discovering the precise nature of the formidable arms arrayed against them did not weaken the Israelis' resolve about the future of their state—on the contrary, the immediate postwar reaction was "Let's recruit more immigrants while Israel's in everybody's mind"—but it did arouse a wave of anger against Russia. For the Arab inefficiencies doubtless would be erased in time, and meanwhile the Russian equipment was in superb fighting condition and was often superior in performance to Western weapons. For example I saw an antitank rocket unit with four missiles capable of penetrating the armor of any known tank and better than anything the West was known to have. A rapid-fire cannon, a radar control for controlling artillery fire on moving targets, an elaborate radio-communications vehicle, and a new recoilless antitank gun were all recent products from Soviet Russian arsenals. Russia's newest howitzer, with a ten-mile range and capable of firing five to seven rounds a minute, would have outperformed any Western equivalent. Stalin tanks, properly handled, should have made mincemeat of the Israeli armor. That none of this sophisticated weaponry helped Egypt was certainly no fault of Russia's.

*   *   *

There were strange rumors about Russian prisoners, said to be held in conditions of great secrecy. Foreign journals began raising questions about the huge number of Egyptian prisoners (5,499 had been counted by June 14) and, perhaps out of a sense of fair play, Israel was accused of displaying an indifference to enemy soldiers lost in the desert. Premier Eshkol was criticized for saying on the first day of war that his country wanted no Arab territory, and then modifying this with suggestions that the military gains would be used to force a peace settlement—as if Israeli "ambitions rose in step with their victories," said the *Economist* of London.

Much of this comment was ill-informed. A staff general, Shmuel Eyal, answered questions about prisoners, and the only doubts raised by foreign observers were about his claim of *no* Russian prisoners. He said nine Egyptian generals and ten colonels had been captured, but it was untrue that Israel was only holding officers as prisoners. Pressed on the matter of prisoners who, it had been rumored, were left to die of thirst, he said Israeli troops had been trying to collect them in vehicles to transport them back to the Canal, adding, "I regret that I saw yesterday a wounded Israeli soldier shot in the stomach while announcing to Arab soldiers they would be treated in accordance with the Geneva Convention."

It was apparent that Israeli forces were taking losses from snipers who refused to admit the war was over. The hands of the authorities were already full with refugees. There was little time to worry about Egyptian soldiers who might repay Israeli concern with a bullet.

The refugees kept bobbing up in the wake of the war. Israel was under a lot of pressure to make room for Arabs who had lost their land. But the government was worried about those already resident, numbering (at an informed guess) close to 250,000 and likely to outbreed the Jews if 300,000 refugees (about a third of the bona fide refugees outside Israel) were admitted, as some Western governments were suggesting.

Some foreign comment on the refugee problem seemed totally unreal to those of us on the spot. Patrick O'Donovan caught the mood of the Israeli dilemma exactly when he described for the *London Observer* the refugee camps which had been overrun. These camps where Palestine Arabs were kept alive by the UN were "festering with hatred, rotten with idleness, victims first of war and then of cynical politics." One of these camps was near Jericho among monasteries celebrating the baptism of Jesus. The place was almost empty. Houses were padlocked. In one night most had fled. "They heard the battle thunder in the hills," wrote O'Donovan. "They saw the remnants of their army stream past. On Wednesday the battle for Jericho itself lasted only an hour . . . They were caught by a fear which is somehow the same as their hatred . . . They took their hopes and hatreds a little deeper into Asia. No damage had been done, no threats made or implied by the Israelis."

The rapid recovery from the scorching of Jerusalem was illustrated by an advertisement calling upon residents to notify the authorities in accordance with a Property Tax and Compensation Fund Law. This appeared in the *Jerusalem Post* of Monday, June 12, and like so many items in that extraordinary issue, it left the reader wondering if he had dreamed the past week. Indeed, there was a Jaffa shopkeeper named Samuel Kohen who had entered a hospital at the end of May for a fairly drastic operation and was not well enough to hear any outside news until the day he opened this particular edition of the *Post*. He wrote later that he felt like a week-old Rip Van Winkle.

The *Post* was only four pages but it mirrored a great deal. A front-page editorial, "Morning After the War," warned against "the hypocritical sequel to the Sinai campaign" being

111

repeated, whereby Israel's "so-called friends as well as her enemies might renew old balance-of-power stratagems." The extent to which Israel would benefit from military victory depended crucially upon her ability to hold her own in other respects—primarily economically. The threat of war and the war itself had cost the country far more than it could afford. "It is in view of this development," said the writer, "that a huge new loan drive has been launched abroad." He examined the nation's financial situation, which was not good, and in this mood of sobriety suggested that Western nations which had sympathized with Israel when she seemed to be in great danger would be indignant now that she refused to give up dearly bought advantages and "revert to the accepted role of victim."

A report from Beirut said Jordan had lost half its army in the fighting, and in a small town near Tel Aviv a couple who had filed a divorce petition wrote to the local rabbinate that "due to the national situation we have made peace too." Wounded Arab soldiers in the Haifa municipal hospital received gift parcels from the Mayor's wife. The Jerusalem West Rotary Club met in the King David Hotel to hear "Mr. R. Braun speak (with slides) on a recent visit to Africa." A display advertisement thanking the Shaare Zedek Hospital staff was signed "The Paratroopers."

Premier Eshkol said the Arab peoples and Israel had spent since 1952 a total of $10 billion on arms. "Had these vast sums been applied to economic and social needs, millions of human beings who are steeped in poverty could by today have enjoyed an appropriate standard of living." He called on Arab leaders to help end the fearful waste of money.

* * *

The school year was extended by ten days, the Ministry of Education announced, having estimated this was roughly how much time the children had lost as a result of the war. Air France announced that flights to Paris would be resumed. The Soviet Embassy in Tel Aviv was put under heavy guard while the staff prepared to leave, diplomatic relations having been broken.

* * *

Some satirical verses in Hebrew appeared in the army journal *Bamahaneh* (*In Camp*) by the poet Dahn ben Amotz. They caught the flavor of what a cockney volunteer called "This Was the Week That Was."

The verses took the form of thanks to:

the aging citizens who shook mothballs from their World War II khakis to work as air-raid wardens and in rescue squads;

schoolchildren who delivered mail because the mailmen had all gone to war;

citizens who paid their income tax five years ahead of time to pay for defense;

ultra-orthodox Jews who were *not* asked to work on the Sabbath before the balloon went up;

housewives who had to clear bomb cellars of cherished relics and junk;

shopkeepers, none of whom yielded to the temptation to hike prices;

workers who gave up vacations and could never now take them;

border security patrols who now had more borders to patrol;

intelligence agents in gray flannel suits who could never answer the question: "What did you do in the war, Daddy?";

good citizens who taped their windows against bomb blast but did it artistically;

police who gave out *no* tickets during the week of war;

ultra-orthodox Jews who worked with bare-arm girls in the fields;

hundreds overseas who couldn't get on planes and arrived when the war was won;

drivers who gave up their thousands of elegant cars and got them back covered in mud and scraped by barbed wire;

taxis which volunteered to run goods to the front lines;

farmers who plowed their fields with a hand on their guns;

actors like Hayim Topol, Israeli star of a London show, who dropped everything to fly home.

"Thank God," he ended, "we can now go back to sitting in the cafés and discotheques, back to our strikes and our protests against desecration of the Sabbath, our constant complaining and libeling of public personalities—in fact, back to being ourselves."

113

CHAPTER FOURTEEN

The war found immediate echoes in the UN, where Secretary-General U Thant heard mounting criticism. Senator Everett Dirksen charged that he "acted like a thief in the night" and there was a chorus about Mr. Thant's "poltroonery" (Joseph Alsop), "dynamism of a noodle" (C. L. Sulzberger), and "collapse" (Barbara Tuchman). Only Paul Martin, the Canadian Foreign Minister, withstood the first barrage and declared Mr. Thant really had no alternative but to withdraw UNEF's troops.

Some critics based a claim that Cairo had no right to insist on withdrawal on a so-called "good-faith understanding" of late 1956. They said the Egyptian advance to the border ended UNEF's buffer role before its withdrawal was requested. They warned against the risk of humiliating disaster if UNEF were kept on Egyptian soil against Egyptian wishes; and that view was substantiated by Nasser when he said UNEF would have been regarded as a hostile force "and forcibly disarmed."

Despite such defense of the UN Secretary-General's case, confidence had been undermined in other UN peacekeeping activities. This was reflected in an interview given by Israel's Foreign Minister Abba Eban after the war: "We must avoid going back to an intermediate situation between war and peace, with all its ambivalence and obscurity." He wanted to stop Arab leaders from believing "international pressure can secure them the kind of victory which eluded them during the war."

*   *   *

Eban and many Israelis who shared his beliefs, including Mrs. Golda Meir, his predecessor, sought some form of union with Jordan which would at once end one major refugee

114

problem, and demonstrate a basic Arab-Jewish ability to cooperate. This dream had been cherished a long time by Eban, who had written:

> Israel's land is small but wonderfully central. It is a nodal point of communication. Imagine roads and railways running from Haifa to Beirut, Damascus and Istanbul in the north; to Amman and beyond in the east; and to Cairo in the south. The opening of these blocked arteries would stimulate the life, thought, and commerce of the region beyond any level conceivable. What is now often described as a wedge between Arab lands would become a bridge.

Unhappily, the Monday morning mood in Israel was not reflected in Cairo. Once again the official Egyptian radio took up the old refrain, echoed in other Arab capitals, that Israel must be destroyed. It seemed incredible.

"I'm afraid the Jews don't hate the Arabs," said an American journalist. "But the Arabs do hate the Jews. That's the trouble in a nutshell."

An old friend and colleague, John Ridley, saw a mutual acquaintance of ours beaten into insensibility by Cairo's plainclothes police. Ridley was forced to leave Egypt shortly afterward and he reported to his newspaper, the *Daily Telegraph,* the dangerous and vengeful state in which Arabs were falling. The victim of police violence was a mild-mannered Egyptian newspaperman I had known for many years, and his intelligent search for some alternative to anti-Jewish hatred had brought him to this tragic pass.

A cold assessment of Israel's position, then, was this. Her forces had cracked the ring of Arab armor but they had stopped short of conquest, and in consequence the Nasserite poison continued to seep through Middle Eastern minds. The lies from Radio Cairo were bigger than ever, the distortions graver, and it was plain that Arabs were once again assuming that words were reality—as they have for centuries in their poetry and prayers. Israel, it turned out, had not won a victory. It was all an Anglo-American imperialist plot. The day of reckoning would come.

Was it possible Arabs might face the truth? Among the 13 member nations of the Arab League (each one declaring its support for Egypt) only three had played any crucial part in the struggle and perhaps only five or six could be immediately expected to help reshape the Middle East, given an end to Nasser-type propaganda.

At the core Egypt still remained. It still had the biggest armed forces, the largest reserves of educated people, the largest industries; about one-third of all the Arabs lived there. Cairo Radio still ranked among the seven most powerful broadcasting stations in the world and it commanded audiences all along the south and east Mediterranean. Its broadcasts continued to reflect Arab humiliations, Arab resentments, and Arab mistrust of the West.

Syria was the scene of the introduction to the war, and Damascus claimed still to be the center of Arab ideas. If Egypt were to collapse from internal strains caused by the war, then Syria could be expected to continue its dangerous course of stirring mischief against Israel. But coups had followed one another with sufficient rapidity to leave some hope that a more moderate regime could emerge. Unfortunately the history of Syria had been one of miscalculations on the part of Syrian nationalists who pursued a dream of Pan-Arab power. President Nureddin Atassi's government had declared a policy of crushing Israel by means of "revolutionary war," and thus maneuvered Nasser into a position of equal belligerence.

Jordan was the most unnatural Arab state and the occupation by Israel of Jerusalem and the West Bank made it possible to talk of an alliance, since King Hussein was in a poor position to do much else. Given his compulsive partnership, Israel could hope to show what might be achieved when her resources of brains and experience were placed at Arab disposal.

Beyond these three, Israel had to consider two large but less pressing neighbors: Saudi Arabia and Iraq. The first had opposed Nasser in Yemen but backed Nasser in the war by suspending oil shipments. King Faisal was the guardian of the Moslem holy places at Mecca and Medina and his religious leadership could command a certain following. He had a massive oil income to free him from pressures by Egypt, and he had the advantage of being a hereditary ruler. But his country was undeveloped and its independence recent, and when the chips were down, Saudi Arabia had joined the others who felt the urgent passion of Arab frustrations. Iraq had been in the forefront of the anti-Israeli campaign and yet it did little more than send troops to Jordan and cut off oil supplies to America and Britain. Its capital of Baghdad was likely to remain, as it had been for a long time, weakened by storms and stresses created by political instability.

Eight other Arab League states and an assortment of sheikhdoms and sultanates would also react to Israel's military actions. Some were significant because of their wealth, some important for their size, and all were likely to be influenced by an ominous development perceived by seasoned observers of the Mideast scene.

This was a widespread withdrawal by the Arabs into their religion. On the morning after the war, for the first time in many years, Cairo broadcast long readings of the Koran in addition to its ritualistic shafts of hate. With revenge in their hearts and the Prophet to purify their determination to destroy the tiny state which had so completely humiliated them, the Arabs seemed only to promise another conflict at a later date. Lawrence of Arabia had said: "There is no record of any force except success capable of breaking them." And by stopping short of total conquest, as practical considerations as much as humanity had forced the Israelis to do, the forces of Israel made it possible for Nasser to assert again that no victory had been won at all.

A young Israeli girl, on that Monday after the war, told her mother she wanted to study Arabic "because I want to be able to talk with the Arabs." But a wise if cynical writer from Italy observed: "It's the Arabs who won't want to talk to her."

The cynicism depressed me until someone pointed out the General Staff had felt a bit depressed too when confronted with the seeming logic of numbers on the eve of war. "We estimated ten days before the weight of the Arabs began to crush our waning reserves," said a staff officer. "I asked a rabbi, 'How do we win?'

" 'By one of two ways,' replied the rabbi. 'By a miracle or by a natural way.'

" 'What would be a natural way?'

" 'To win by a miracle.'

" 'And what would be a miracle?'

" 'To win,' said the rabbi, 'by a natural way.' "

Flying over the shattered Arab armor on what might have been Day Zero, I reflected that the Israelis had achieved a miracle by their natural courage. What happened in the week June 5 to June 12 was in microcosm what would confront

117

us all. A nation incapable of hating its enemies broke off an action which could have destroyed them entirely. Could such a people survive in a world where generosity of spirit is still regarded as weakness? Already the pessimists talked of another clash with the Arabs within ten years. But if it took a week to achieve this miracle below my wings by a natural way, surely ten years was not too long to wait for a miracle.

June 20, 1967
Tel Aviv

THE THIRD TEMPLE

BY LEON URIS

T HE superlatives heaped upon Israel's victorious forces have a black counterpoint. The new praise can only be matched by the old eternal scorn and defilement borne by the Jewish people.

As the world gasped in awe at the furiosity and precision of Israel's "terrible swift sword," those who record the passing scene flooded the media with millions of words of succinct observations, erudite rhetoric, and handy biblical quotations to fill all occasions. Yet, conspicuous by its absence is what really astonished everyone the most. For two thousand years we Jews have been characterized and libeled as a race of cowards and cunning shylocks.

This stunning military victory was planned by Jewish generals and achieved by Jewish flyers, Jewish tank drivers and gunners, Jewish paratroops, Jewish artillery, Jewish infantry, Jewish reserves.

The lie has been put to rest for all time. It will never be the same, for from this day forward the word "Jew" will not be used again as a slander.

The Bible did not really end with Malachi or Revelation, for this odyssey of the Jews is unique in all of man's history and has closed a sweeping circle of six thousand years.

I could never be mistaken for either a Talmudic scholar or a classical author but, nonetheless, I should like to humbly speculate about some of the sounds and content on the continuation, which I should like to call "Book of the Return."

Book of the Return

No people ever fought with more valor for their freedom than the Hebrews to keep their Covenant with God. Such deeds are recorded through the story of the Maccabees, who arose against Hellenistic attempts to profane their Temple. Judah Maccabee, called "the Hammer," led a small band, greatly outnumbered by the Syrians. With Messianic fervor we exhorted them with the battle cry, "Be zealous of the Law, and give your lives for the Covenant of your fathers!" Jerusalem was conquered, the statue to Zeus was destroyed, and the Temple rededicated in the Feast of Lights, later to be known as Hanukkah. After eighty years the tyrants of Rome returned with their legions under the direction of Pompey and there was a massacre of tens of thousands. But the Jews would not accept the oppression of Rome and continued to foment anarchy until they rose again in full-scale rebellion. Under the leadership of Simon bar Giora and Johanan of Giscala, the Zealot bands reconquered David's city of Jerusalem.

The Romans besieged the city without mercy. When loss of might and disease and hunger made resistance against Titus no longer possible, Jerusalem fell on the ninth day of the month of Ab and rivers of blood were spilled by maniacal Roman butchery in the streets. And the great Temple was destroyed by fire, with many Zealots choosing to burn alive therein. Simon bar Giora was skinned alive and Johanan of Giscala was made to walk through the streets of Rome in chains, and a coin was struck bearing the words *"Judaea capta"*—"The Jews are defeated."

But the Hebrew Zealots fought on.

A century earlier, Herod had built a retreat on a flat-topped mountain called the Masada, which stood near the Dead Sea. It was here that Ben Eliezer came with less than two hundred Zealot men, women, and children. For over two years they withstood the siege and assaults of a Roman legion. When, at last, the end was inevitable, Ben Eliezer called his people to him and told them they were never to be paraded through the streets of Rome as slaves. And they agreed. They had kept faith with God and the principles of liberty and would die like free men and women.

Each man was assigned to kill his wife and children. When this was done, they drew lots to find ten executioners of the others. Each man lay beside his family, embraced them, and bared his throat for his comrade to slaughter him. When this was done they drew lots again and one man was chosen to kill the remaining nine.

Then, he drove his sword through his body and fell at the side of his wife.

And the Jews made more rebellions in Egypt and Cyprus and Mesopotamia and elsewhere in the Empire and these too were crushed.

But the Jews fought on.

A century later, a new Roman tyrant, Hadrian, invoked harsh edicts against the Jews in order to deny them their religion, and Hadrian set forth to create a heathen city of Jerusalem and rename it "Aelia Capitolina" and build a temple to Jupiter.

And the Jews rebelled.

Led by Bar-Kochba, all of the Kingdom of Judah was liberated and Jerusalem was captured after the total defeat of a Roman legion. Attempts to put down the revolution by the Governor of Syria failed. Hadrian was forced to recall his greatest general, Julius Severus, from Britain, and place him at the head of legions gathered from all over the Empire.

Faced with overwhelming might a half hundred Jewish bastions fell, one by one, fighting to the last man as was their tradition. And a thousand villages were leveled to the ground and women and children were taken to slavery. Again the rivers of blood ran deep and swift from a million slaughtered Jews. Bar-Kochba fell in the fortress of Bethar south of Jerusalem on the ninth day of Ab, a day of catastrophe in Jewish history. This time the Jewish nation was crushed and the survivors were cast to the four corners of the earth as cursed exiles and eternal wanderers.

And all that remained was the Western Wall of the Second Temple.

1

Where they don't wear pants,
   In the southern part of France,
But the things they do,
   Are enough to kill a Jew . . .

A children's song repeated over and over tauntingly in the yard of the Jeb Stuart Grammar School in Norfolk, Virginia. There were other rhymes in other schoolyards in Baltimore and Philadelphia for me and for my children in San Francisco and Los Angeles. They all promised death to the Jews.

We were the only Jewish family in our neighborhood in Norfolk. I was called "Little Jew" and my stepbrother, "Big Jew." About once every two weeks, for reasons I never learned, I'd find myself looking into a dozen angry faces of kids I played with who were trying to trap me. I'd be called "kike" and "sheeny" and someone would put a chip on his shoulder and dare me to knock it off. If I didn't, he'd put it on my shoulder and flick it to the ground and everyone would say, "Little Jew started it." I had to become a fairly good fighter and every now and then I'd be winning one. It didn't pay because I'd have three or four more kids to fight if I won, sometimes all of them at once. At other times, when they were in these moods, I'd get caught alone and catch a rock barrage. There was nothing much to do but turn tail and hide in the basement. There were always too many of them.

At Grammar School 62 in Baltimore a pal of mine had a swastika carved on his cheek with a penknife. It took a lot of them to hold him down. But there were always a lot of them.

I remember one particular night when I was in the Marine Corps in Camp McKay, New Zealand. A half dozen of my buddies came in drunk from liberty and decided to have a little fun with the Jewish guy in the next tent.

I could hear what was going on as I lay in my cot. The oaths, the profanities. They said they were fighting the war to make Jews like him rich. This didn't make much sense because he was a poor slum boy. They dumped him, gave him a shock of ice water, and scattered his gear outside and roughed him up. I didn't do anything but lie still. In those days I didn't admit to being a Jew. I'd gotten mine in boot camp when I became enraged and it took four of them to knock me cold. But there were always four of them.

So, how do you even the score? Slide into second base a little harder and try to spike the ankles. Hike without asking for relief even though your feet are bleeding. Keep trying to prove to yourself and them you are a man and you aren't different than anyone else.

But they make you different because they won't leave you alone.

Men get scared in combat. That's human. But by the time bullets were being fired at you a hundred incidents in your growing up had made you believe that you were scared for one reason . . . that you were a Jew and you were different. It had been ingrained that being a Jew made you a coward.

In America, for the most part, we were asked to endure the more "polite" forms of antisemitism. But polite or otherwise the "J" was branded on your heart in such a way that sometimes you carried it as a badge of shame.

Book of the Return

In the places of their exile the Jews were to suffer unspeakable persecution. Some lived in walled cities, forcibly separated from normal life. In most places they were not allowed to own land or practice trades and professions and were kept from obtaining an education. Some were forced by torture to deny their religion and convert or face imprisonment or death. Century after century the catalogue of abuses grew, to stagger the sensibilities of sane men.

2

"Hab-hab!" chanted blood-crazed German mobs in the Middle Ages. At the time of the Crusades, massacres destroyed Jewish communities in Cologne and Worms and Mainz and dozens of other cities.

The Crusaders continued their "holy" works when they captured Jerusalem and burned the Jews alive in their own synagogue after a massacre over the length and breadth of Palestine.

The Second, Third, Fourth, and Fifth Crusades continued the "noble" quests, goaded by papal oils on the fire, until the wholesale slaughter of defenseless Jews was common sport all over Europe.

The "Christ killers" were segregated into ghettos, strangled economically, and accused of ritual murder, causing the black plague, and just about every other calamity of the times.

We are blamed for fostering capitalism through a world conspiracy of Jewish bankers and we are blamed for fostering communism, as arch-enemies of the capitalists. We are blamed for a Zionist conspiracy by the survivors of Hitlerism and we are called Nazis by the Russians. Sometimes, it just doesn't pay to wake up in the morning if it's raining too hard. Next day the sun may be too hot and when you're responsible for all those things it's hard to win.

The "official" Dark Ages fell on Europe. Indeed, it was

difficult to tell just when the Dark Ages began or ended for the Jews. There were mass expulsions from almost every land, including the "enlightened" countries of England and France.

The Inquisition was dictated by the Dominican priest, Tomás de Torquemada, who was outraged by his own part-Jewishness. It was convert or die. Deny your God or be burned alive at the stake. The affluent Jewish community of Spain were called Marranos—"pigs"—and when the Inquisition's frenzy passed the Jews were expelled from Spain and fled to Portugal only to be expelled from Portugal to flee again.

The Reformation. Martin Luther firebranded his own new form of Christianity and it swept the German lands. After Luther made it simple for the Jews to convert, he was confounded by their unwillingness to break their Covenant and he called for the destruction of Jewish synagogues, confiscation of Jewish property, and expulsion.

In the countries to the east, they had their own word for Jew killing, "pogrom" . . . a word known by my father and my grandfather. In Poland, Russia, and the Baltic and Slavic nations, brutal persecution never began or ended but only continued unabated from the Cossack massacres to the Black Hundreds of Russia.

Book of the Return

The Jews never stopped looking to their ancient homeland and dreaming of the Western Wall of the Temple. Their anguished prayers throughout their exile ended always with the words "Next year in Jerusalem."

Despite the catastrophes, they kept the faith. The honored among their communities were the learned men. Despite their small numbers, they never failed to enrich their adopted countries. The list of great scientists and musicians and writers and artists and physicians and merchants and scholars was utterly without end. Over fifty of their number were to receive awards in Scandinavia, the highest acclaim man can give his fellow man.

The Jews were to give to the world men who shaped its thought and destiny. Among them was Jesus Christ.

And Einstein and Freud and Heine and Spinoza and Philo and Maimonides and Marx and Rothschild.

One must wonder how terribly empty this world would have been, had it been a world without Jews.

126

The Jew will flee again to a new land and here he will find a freedom he has never known and he will flourish and he will call it "home."

3

It is my personal belief that Zionism is a historical necessity. Israel is the object of much love and affection. But, above that, Israel is *needed*. If the Jews of Russia, Spain, or Yemen had been afforded the same freedoms we have in America, the longing for Israel would not be so acute.

There is a great concern by the leaders of Israel over the lack of substantial immigration from America. I am asked, "What if America turns on the Jews as has happened everywhere else? What then?"

If such a thing were to happen in America then Israel is not the answer for me. I would not want to go on living. There are no questions here of split loyalty. My identity as an American is total. I love my country as much as the Israeli loves his. I would no more put Israel ahead of America than John Kennedy would have put the Vatican ahead of America. I am what I am because my father was sensible enough to catch the boat and God only knows what would have happened if he hadn't.

On the other hand, I will not turn my back on my fellow Jews whose fathers were not as sensible as mine. I do not understand that there is any conflict in supporting the right of my fellow Jews to their own nation and my being a citizen of this country.

4

In 1956 I lived with my family in a small settlement north of Tel Aviv, bordering the Sharon Valley. After many months of travel and research around Israel I began work on *Exodus*. A crisis was heightening. In the Gaza Strip and along the Jordanian and Syrian borders gangs of Arab Fedayeen thugs crossed into Israel nightly raiding Jewish settlements. Then a massive buildup of Russian-supplied Egyptian armor crossed the Sinai to positions on Israel's Negev Desert.

Our home was close to an area called "the bottleneck," so named because the country was scarcely ten miles wide at this point. This unnatural boundary was a leftover of the armistice line of the 1948–1949 War of Liberation—a great bulge from Jordan which almost reached the sea. One night in October I could see the sky aglow with shellfire on the border as Israel was compelled to make a reprisal raid.

The tension thickened and it appeared that a full-scale war could not be far off.

Over Kol Israel radio code words were given in Hebrew and men disappeared from the streets and farms and offices to assemble in hidden places to take up arms and move to the borders. In sad grandeur the country mobilized in silence, each man having his prearranged place of duty.

And war came.

I was warned by the American Embassy to evacuate my family and in deference to our worried relatives back in the States, we decided it would be best. My wife, a former Marine like me, packed two old Marine Corps seabags and we found our way to Lydda Airdrome in total darkness. Inside the terminal there was a scene of monumental confusion and dragging, tension-filled hours of waiting ensued. As the night wore on our three youngsters slept on the two seabags. Rumors, of course, ran rampant. Finally, near dawn, a number of large American transport planes arrived from German bases.

When my oldest son, who was then barely six years of age, discovered I was not going to leave Israel with him . . . he cried. I tried to explain to him that as a writer I had certain duties and I had to honor them. My duty now was to stay in Israel and write about what was going on. He didn't understand.

Then I took him outside to the edge of the apron where the transport planes were parked and I pointed to the Globe-masters. I told him, "You're lucky to be an American, Mark. Think of it. Your country thinks so much of one little boy they would send a big airplane halfway around the world to take him home."

In the backlash of World War II there were other refugee stations in Vienna and Milan and Marseilles carrying out the pathetic survivors of my people. In the darkness of many nights, many little boys must have cried out the horror of their nightmares. There were no planes there to take them home. There was no home . . . except Israel.

This is the meaning of Israel, to move heaven and earth to take every little boy to the only home that wants him.

Am I less of an American for believing in Israel and loving

128

Israel for this? How else can I repay my gratitude to my own country which gave refuge to my father and gave me dignity and identity . . . than to support with all my soul the only place which will give refuge and identity and dignity to other human beings.

5

In the spring of 1964, I had come to England to defend myself against a libel suit brought by a man once wanted as a war criminal. His name was Dr. Wladyslaw Dering. He was a Pole who had been interned in Auschwitz and became one of the principal prisoner-doctors in that dreaded place. As such, he inherited a great deal of power from the Nazis.

Dering took part in heinous medical experiments, taking the testicles from Jewish male victims and the ovaries from females in a most brutal manner. The master plan was to find means to sterilize the Jews so they could be used solely as slaves without the ability to procreate.

I mentioned Dering by name in *Exodus*.

After a number of bizarre postwar happenings, Dering fled to England and managed to escape extradition as a war criminal. He disappeared to British Somaliland and practiced in a hospital. So complete was his "rehabilitation" that many years later he was named OBE—Officer of the British Empire, a reward for outstanding civil service usually granted on the Queen's birthday.

Dering returned to London and resumed his practice there to discover he had been named by me in my novel. He brought suit for libel. It was to become the longest libel trial in British history, known as the "British War Crimes Trial" and fought in eleven languages with thirty-five witnesses we had gathered from around the world.

My chief barrister, Lord Gerald Gardiner, is the greatest man I have ever known. He is a Quaker of the highest moral stature. As a member of the ambulance corps of the British Army he was among the first to enter and liberate Bergen-Belsen, an event that left an indelible scar on his soul.

A few years earlier, when the case was still in a dubious stage, I had gone to him with the most sketchy evidence. We spoke in his tiny office on King's Bench Walk in the ancient Temple area of the barristers . . . a cornerstone of Western thought and justice. Gardiner examined the few documents of evidence and knew the reality of the long hard road ahead. He smiled and in typical understatement said in a soft voice, "Well, we can't let him get away with it, can we?"

On the day our defense began, he arose and walked to the rostrum and opened his notes in an aged, paneled high-ceilinged dark room. He was an extremely tall man—seemingly taller, for he was thin—and had been described as a tombstone with eyes. He made few gestures of any sort. His voice was calm, even, and meticulous.

"It is easy for us, sitting in comfortable England, to criticize what people did or did not do in the situation of that kind—but could any of us be sure how we would have acted in similar conditions?

". . . Where in the world is the most civilized and cultured group of countries? It would show no disrespect for the United States or our own Commonwealth to say, 'Really it is the Christian countries of Western Europe which are the flower of civilization and culture—the highest point which man has yet developed.' And if anyone had asked, 'Do you think it is possible that within relatively few years one of these countries will drive millions of old people and children literally naked into gas chambers?' everybody would have said, 'Absolutely impossible.' In Germany, after all, the Kaiser had gone and all that militarism, and they had an ordinary, Western democratic government. And we should have said, should we not, 'Impossible' for two reasons. First, one cannot conceive of any reason why anybody should do this. They would bring on themselves the loathing of the world for a generation. If they did it in a peacetime situation, they would soon be at war, because everybody would go to stop them. If they did it in a wartime situation, what could they possibly have to gain to justify conduct of that kind and the opprobrium it would bring—and rightly—for a generation? And secondly, we should have said, 'You'll never get the people to do it.' After all, a conscript army is made up of people from homes and factories, who have women and children of their own. Can you imagine that you would ever get men with children of their own to drive children in tens of thousands into gas chambers?

"If it had been said or suggested that, on top of that, human beings would be used as guinea pigs, and have their sexual

130

organs removed literally in front of their eyes while they were conscious, as experiments to see whether men and women could be sterilized en masse, again we would have said, 'It is impossible—and apart from that, a thing like that could only be done by doctors, and where could you find any doctors to do it.'

"Well, we'd have been wrong—because there was a doctor, an antisemitic Polish doctor, the present plaintiff, Dr. Dering, who did it. And if I say 'a' doctor it is because, on the evidence, it is pretty clear that with his dominating position in the hospital and his dominating personality, it really depended on him, on Dr. Dering. As Dr. Grabczynski* had said, 'Of course, if Dr. Dering had refused to do it, I should have refused to do it.'

"Why would we have been wrong? For two reasons. First, there was a cause which was thought to justify it: antisemitism. We ourselves believed that men and women had qualities different from any other created being. Members of religions would say, 'This is only because men and women have souls'; while those who had no religious beliefs might say, 'It is because their intellect is developed to a point wholly different from that of any other creature and they have the ability to recognize the difference between right and wrong, and free will.'

"But, of course, if once you allowed yourself to think that there was some body of men who, because of their race or color, were not really human beings, then you were justified in imposing every sort of disability on them—very useful to rulers, who if they found anything going wrong, could lay it at their doors—the universal scapegoat. If once you thought that you were justified in treating such groups as if they were animals, and said, 'Well, we slaughter animals'—then Auschwitz was simply the logical end of that particular road.

"The second reason why we should have been wrong was that when it came to the point there were not enough people who refused to obey orders to drive children into gas chambers—and old people—who had done nothing except to be the children of their parents. There were people who said: 'I'm not going to do this and live, because I would not like to live and have this on my conscience. I'm not going to do

---

* Dr. Grabczynski was an accomplice in the experiments with Dering and is currently living and practicing in Poland without having ever been brought to trial.

131

it and then say, "Well, I was acting under orders." I am not going to push them into gas chambers and then say, "Well, they're going to be pushed into gas chambers anyhow. I can't stop that. The other people would probably do it much more cruelly. I shall do it much more kindly, and, therefore, it is really in their interest that I should do it rather than these other people." ' The trouble was that when it came to the point there were not enough of such people.

". . . Could the jury imagine any doctor of any sort of humanity at all—however antisemitic he was, and even though these were Jewish patients, if he really thought that there was a medical justification . . . [say] 'It's in your own interest you should have this out, and it's a very good thing for you that it's coming out.'* Dr. Dering agreed that he never suggested that to a patient at all . . .

". . . Then, there was Dr. Hautval, a deeply religious French Protestant. She, being a woman of courage and character, told the Gestapo exactly what she thought about the way they were treating Jews, so they said, 'Oh, well, if that is what you think,' and pinned a thing on her saying *Amie des juifs*'—'Friend of the Jews'—and said, 'Well, if you are so fond of them, you can go to Auschwitz with them'; and she had to go . . .

". . . The trouble was that there were not enough Dr. Hautvals."

At the end of almost a month of the most horrendous testimony ever heard in a British court, Lord Gardiner spoke again in his closing speech.

"The jury has listened patiently to a story that history would describe as what the Christians did to the Jews in Western Europe in the twentieth century. Nowhere in all history was there a blacker picture. That was antisemitism that was!"

Dr. Dering won his case. I was unable to prove the number of "experiments in surgery" I had accused him of and therefore I had libeled him. It was a Pyrrhic victory, indeed. For the defamation of his character he was awarded damages of one halfpenny. He died a year later of stomach cancer.

Lord Gardiner was later named Lord Chancellor of England. It is my belief that he will go down in history as one of the greatest jurists the world has ever known.

* That is, removal of testicles and ovaries.

And so it happened that in a golden age of mankind in a nation of great enlightenment they were to impose upon the Jews the time of the Holocaust. Jews and their children and their elders and their wives were thrown alive into concrete cells and the cells filled with poison fumes. In their agony of agonies they cried, "Oh God, why have we been forsaken!" When the fumes suffocated them to death, the gold was taken from their teeth, the hair from their heads, and the fat from their tissues. They were burned in ovens and their bones crushed by mallet and machine.

6

Dachau is a pleasant place these days. I remember the neatly clipped lawns, the flower-lined paths, and the precise signs and scrubbed buildings. The stench of death had been removed. A few "good" Germans came and placed a bouquet at the statue of the martyr or stood stunned or shed a tear or two. Dachau is a dog scratching to cover its dung.

Maidanek, outside Lublin, in Poland, is not so cheerful. Perhaps the Poles are closer to what really happened. It has been left as the Nazis left it, unscrubbed. It was a lesser extermination camp without the sophisticated assembly-line death methods of Auschwitz.

I entered the gas chamber. It was a small, compact room, of thick solid concrete except for the iron door and the window where the SS observed the gassings. It is a lie that the Jews died quietly. The low concrete ceiling was permanently colored in blood and several inches of it had been clawed away near the door by the victims in a last frenzied crush to live.

The shock of the Holocaust let every living Jew know this could have been him, his mother, his children except for the fortunate miracle of being in another country. The icy chill that swept through all of us was a near-fatal blow to our manliness. We had reached the bottom, the swill pit. The lowest moment in six thousand years of tortured history.

Writers, intellectuals, and learned men tried to explain away and even glorify the manner in which pacifist "Godlike"

133

Jews went to their death in silence. These apologetics, these verbal gymnastics were a final indignity and lie. They did not see the clawed-away concrete at Maidanek.

Book of the Return

At the height of the Cossack atrocities the Jews began to trickle back to Palestine in small numbers at the turn of the twentieth century. The land, once called milk and honey, had grown fallow from neglect. Those who now inhabited it were lethargic, the cities decayed, the culture stagnant. The magnificent terraces of the Judean hills, which once gave life to hundreds of thousands, were wasted with erosion; the fertile valleys of Galilee had diminished to festering swamps; and the desert was a baked wilderness. Those Jewish pioneers who dared it toiled beyond all human measure to redeem and to build and to bring light in a place where there had only been darkness. The redemption of the ancient land became a saga of the human spirit.

There was a great council of all the nations and there was a moment of miracle. In a gesture of atonement it was declared by the nations that Israel should be reborn as a sovereign state among the peoples . . . two thousand years after the fall of the Second Temple and the revolutions.

But once having so made the declaration, the infant state was abandoned. From all of her borders came the ancient cry, "Kill the Jews . . . perish Judea." The new state was small and had very little in the way of arms but they were brave and they had within them the ancient tradition and they beat back the intruders and gained an armistice.

But a scar ran over the land. A no-man's zone split Jerusalem and the Jews were denied the right to return to the most holy of places, the Western Wall of the Temple.

And each day threats of destruction were rained on them. But they turned to creating an oasis in the desert.

(From my novel *Exodus*, Book Five, "With Wings as Eagles,"
Chapter Two)

The trickle became a stream and then a deluge of humanity.

The exodus soon doubled, then began to triple, the population of Israel. The economy, ruptured by the War of Liberation, buckled under the flood of immigrants. Many came with little more than the clothes they were wearing. Many were old and many were ill and many were illiterate, but no matter what the condition, no matter what the added burden, no Jew was turned away from the doors of Israel.

It was not a melting pot, it was a pressure cooker, for they came from every corner of the earth and had lived under every variety of circumstance.

Tent cities and ugly corrugated-tin-shack villages sprang up to blot the landscape from the Galilee to the Negev. Hundreds of thousands of people lived "under canvas," in makeshift hovels, breaking down the medical, educational, and welfare facilities.

Yet there was an attitude of optimism all over the land. From the moment the downtrodden set foot on the soil of Israel they were granted a human dignity and freedom that most of them had never known, and this equality fired them with a drive and purpose without parallel in man's history.

Cities and towns seemed to spring up from the earth.

South Africans and South Americans and Canadians poured money into industry. Factories were built until the manufacturing potential reached one of the highest levels in Africa or Asia. General scientific, medical, and agricultural research reached an advanced stage.

Tel Aviv expanded into a bustling metropolis of a quarter of a million people, and later a half million. Haifa grew into one of the most important ports on the Mediterranean. In both cities, heavy industry sprang up. New Jerusalem, the capital and educational center of the new nation, expanded into the hills.

Chemicals, drugs, medicines, mining, engineering, shoe and clothing manufacturing—the list grew into thousands of items. Cars were assembled and buses were built. Tires were made and airstrips laid down, and a network of highways spanned the nation.

Housing, housing, housing—people needed homes, and the concrete and steel skylines pushed farther into the suburbs almost by the hour. The sound of the hammer, the music of the drill, the concrete mixer, the welding torch never stopped in Israel!

The arts flourished. Bookstores lined Herzl Street and Allenby Road. In every kibbutz and in every home and in every moshev shelves were filled with books written in a dozen languages. Musicians, painters, writers put this dynamic new society into words and on canvas and into melody.

From Metulla to Elath, from Jerusalem to Tel Aviv there was the electrifying feel and smell of one huge boom town.

The Negev Desert composed half the area of Israel. It was for the most part a wilderness, with some areas which resembled the surface of the moon. This was the wilderness of Paran and Zin where Moses wandered in search of the Promised Land. It was a broiling mass of denuded desolation where the heat burned down at 125 degrees over the endless slate fields and deep gorges and canyons. Mile after mile of the rock plateaus would not give life to so much as a single blade of grass. No living thing, not even a vulture, dared penetrate.

The Negev became Israel's challenge. The Israelis went down to the desert! They lived in merciless heat and they built settlements on rock. They did as Moses had done: they brought water from the rocks, and they made life grow.

They searched for minerals. Potash was pulled from the Dead Sea. King Solomon's copper mines, silent for eternities, were made to smelt the green ore again. Traces of oil were found. A mountain of iron was discovered. The northern entrance to the Negev, Beersheba, the city of Abraham, became a new city with a skyline springing up on the desert overnight.

Life in Israel was brutally hard. It was a poor and unfertile country and every single advance was made with sweat. Workers labored exhausting hours for little pay. Those out in the settlements fighting the soil toiled under nearly unbearable conditions. All the citizens were taxed to the breaking point to pay for the new immigrants pouring in. Clawing, bleeding, conquering with their bodies and minds, they made the tiny nation live and grow.

A national airline took to the skies.

A merchant marine flying the Star of David began to sail to the corners of the earth.

The people forged ahead with a determination that captured the heart of the civilized world. Young Israel stood out as a lighthouse for all mankind, proving what could be done with will power and love. No one in Israel worked for comfort in his own lifetime: it was all for tomorrow, for the children, for the new immigrant coming in. And in the wake of this drive, the tough young sabra generation emerged, a generation never to know humiliation for being born a Jew.

Israel became an epic in the history of man.

8

I wept openly as I walked over the martyred grounds of the ruins of the Warsaw ghetto, that vile walled pesthole that gave death to a half million Jews at the hands of the Nazis.

But yet I was warmed with pride, for in the end a few hundred rebelled as they had rebelled at Bethar and Masada.

It was here, in the depth of Jewish agony, that the Star of David was raised and flew over free men in an epic struggle which foretold the coming of Israel.

This rabble army of Jews held at bay the German military power for forty-two days and forty-two nights. It did not seem possible, for all of Poland had been able to hold for less than a month in 1939 and other nations had been trampled under the German juggernaut in days.

Those who fought kept faith with the ancient tradition to defend the "laws." The uprising of the Warsaw ghetto was the link in the chain from the glorious past to the glorious future.

9

(From my novel *Exodus*, concerning my beliefs on the mission of Israel)

A young girl named Karen who had lost her family in the Holocaust and had made her way to Israel on a refugee ship went by choice to live in a new border settlement in the desert in the face of obvious danger from the Arabs. An American gentile nurse named Kitty, who loved her as her own, went to visit her.

Kitty had traveled over most of Israel and she had seen the most rugged of the settlements. She knew when she traveled to Nahal Midbar that it was the brink of hell. Yet in spite of

137

preparing herself for the worst her heart sank at the sight of Nahal Midbar, a bake furnace planted in the path of angry Arab hordes.

Karen showed Kitty around with obvious pride over what had been accomplished in three months. There were a few new wooden shacks, a few more dunams of land plowed, but it was a heartbreaking sight. It represented boys and girls working agonizing hours during the day and standing guard during the night.

"In a few years," Karen said, "there will be trees and flowers everywhere, if we can only get enough water."

They walked out of the sun into Karen's hospital tent and each had a drink of water. Kitty looked through the tent flap. Barbed wire and trenches. Out in the fields, boys and girls worked in the sun while others walked behind them with rifles, guarding them. One hand on the sword and one on the plow. That was the way they had rebuilt the walls of Jerusalem in ancient times. Kitty looked at Karen. The girl was so young and so lovely. In a few years in this place she would age before her time. . . .

They were silent for a long time. The flies swarmed around Kitty. She spun around quickly and faced Karen. "I can't go without telling you I am sick about your coming to this place."

"The borders must be defended. It is easy enough to say let the other fellow do it."

"Nahal Midbar is three months old. Already you have a boy and girl in your graveyard, murdered by Fedayeen."

"We don't think of it that way, Kitty. Two are lost but fifty more have joined Nahal Midbar and another fifty have come to build a settlement five kilometers away—because we came here. In a year we will have a children's house and a thousand dunams of land under cultivation."

"And in a year you will begin to grow old. You will work eighteen hours a day and spend your nights in the trenches. All that you will ever have is a single room eight by ten feet. Even the clothes on your back won't belong to you."

"You are wrong, Kitty. I will have everything."

"Including a quarter of a million kill-crazy Arabs at your throats."

"We cannot be angry at those poor people," Karen said. "They sit there day after day, month after month, locked up like animals, watching our fields grow green."

Kitty sagged down on a cot and buried her face in her hands.

138

"Kitty . . . listen . . ."

"I can't."

"Please . . . please listen. You know that even when I was a little girl in Denmark I asked myself why I was born a Jew. I know the answer now. God didn't ask us because we were weak or would run from danger. We've taken murder and sorrow and humiliation for six thousand years and we have kept faith. We have outlived everyone who has tried to destroy us. Can't you see it? This little land was chosen for us because it is the crossroads of the world, on the edge of man's wilderness. Where else is there for us to be?"

"Israel stands with its back to the wall," Kitty cried. "It has always stood that way and it always will . . . with enemies trying to destroy you."

"Oh no, Kitty, no! Israel is the bridge between darkness and light."

And suddenly Kitty saw it all so clearly . . . so beautifully clear. This then was the answer. Israel, the bridge between darkness and light.

10

David Ben-Gurion said the Jews did not believe it when Hitler threatened to exterminate them. He also said, "When Nasser said it, we believed him."

Let us put to rest the Arab mythology that they have lived in peace, side by side with the Jew as their brother, as they now claim. I should say, in all fairness, they have never matched the refined genocide of the Germans.

But it is a hashish dream that the Arab ever allowed the Jew to live as an equal in any Arab land. The usual abuses were all there beginning with "holy wars" against the Jews led by no less than Mohammed, himself.

One has only to look at a map to understand the warped Arab logic of "Israel's aggression" and "Zionist plots," but the "big lie" has been so often repeated that this phobia, this tragic welding point for Arab unity has become what they really believe.

If Israel had lost this war it would have been their last war.

Today, no Arab city lies in ruins.

No Arab capital is occupied.

Make no mistake about who fired the first shot. The Arabs never stopped firing the last one.

It was the Arabs who imposed a state of war for twenty years.

It was the Arabs who refused to come to the peace table.

It was the Arabs who denied Israel use of the Suez Canal.

It was the Arabs who raided the borders for two decades and murdered farmers in their fields.

It was the Arabs who bankrupted their economy with the bankrupt ideology of an arms race.

It was the Arabs who denied the Jews their holy places of worship in Jerusalem.

It was the Arabs who blocked the Strait of Tiran.

It was the Arabs who spewed venom for twenty years promising to obliterate Israel, to destroy its cities, to plow under its farms, to throw its people into the sea.

It was the Egyptian dictator who willingly took up the baton of Adolf Hitler, hired escaped Nazis, some directly from Goebbels' propaganda machine, and vowed to finish the job of genocide.

11

I remember the purple glow of dawn on the desert at the demarcation line near the Suez Canal during the Sinai War of 1956. I was by a radio jeep as the news was broadcast over Kol Israel radio. Ben-Gurion was speaking. (You see, I'm not a very good Jew because I don't speak Hebrew, nor have I been bar-mitzvahed, so I asked for a translation.)

"What did the Old Man say?" I asked.

"Just a quotation from the Bible," the radio operator answered. "Isaiah, chapter nineteen."

There was, of course, a Bible close by and I read . . . "The Lord hath mingled a perverse spirit in the midst of it; and they have caused Egypt to err in every work of it, as a drunken man staggereth in his vomit . . . In that day shall Egypt be like a woman; and it shall be afraid and fear because of the shaking of the hand of the Lord of hosts, which he shaketh over it."

12

My family name is Yerushalmi in Hebrew. Translated, it means "Man from Jerusalem."

I have two first cousin Yossi's in Israel. One was an officer in the paratroops in the first Sinai War of 1956 and fought at Mitla Pass. The other Yossi is also a paratrooper and was in the front of the battle for the Old City of Jerusalem. My cousins Zev and Moche and Yacov and Serfi were in the thick of it.

They are good boys . . . good soldiers . . . almost as good as Marines.

13

I have seen miracles. From the lowest point in our history, we Jews have risen to the highest point in our history in a mere twenty-five years. From the Holocaust of World War II to the victorious battles for freedom in Israel.

The world has seen the last generation of Jews to ever go to their deaths without fighting.

If there is one miracle, one wish, one prayer, it would be for peace and for the Arab leaders to see the light. A cancer of hate and disease and hunger and ignorance blights their land.

The Jews of Israel can and will bring light to the Arabs. May God give them the wisdom to receive it.

Book of the Return

And so they fought three wars for freedom in two decades. In the end, the Jews stood alone. As in the beginning they were few but they were brave. And they crushed the enemies all around them with such swiftness that all men in all places stood in awe. It did not seem that this was an army of mortals.

And the terrible odyssey was over. Never again would the Jews have to wail in anguish, "Next year in Jerusalem."

As in the glorious times of kings and prophets, great new warriors and rabbis and scholars had risen among them.

And when the third and final war was done they went up into their ancient capital. Many of them had dropped the names of their exile and taken ancient names. Ben-Gurion and Dayan and Rabin and Meir and Eban.

And they stood before the Western Wall of the Temple and prayed and danced and they wept for joy.

And the Lord felt they had kept the faith well and suffered enough. And he bade them build a third Temple and dwell in their own land, forever.

June 20, 1967
New York City

PORTFOLIO PHOTOGRAPHS IN ORDER OF APPEARANCE

Israeli tanks on the alert: © Newsphot, Ltd.—Pictorial Parade
President Nasser's press conference, June 4, 1967: Paris-Match
Arab civilians demonstrating for war: Paris-Match
Palestine Liberation Army troops ready for battle: A.F.P. from Pictorial
Arab soldier's family farewell: Camera Press—Pix
Egyptian pilot prepared for action: Camera Press—Pix
Israeli tank crew: Werner Braun for Camera Press—Pix
Israeli armored forces in the Negev: Werner Braun for Camera Press—Pix
Israeli soldier-performers entertain comrades: © Newsphot, Ltd.—Pictorial Parade
Old and young dig in for Israel defense: Central Press
Israeli girl soldier: Pictorial Parade
Israeli girl soldier: Pictorial Parade
Israeli jets at war: Central Press
Battle action in Jordan: Gamma-Pix
Victorious Israeli troops roll into El Arish: London Daily Express
Battle-weary Israeli machine-gunner: Don McCullen for Camera Press—Pix
Israeli troops climb toward Mandelbaum Gate: Gamma-Pix
Israeli soldiers entering old Jerusalem: Don McCullen for Camera Press—Pix
Israeli soldiers under sniper fire: Don McCullen for Camera Press—Pix
Arabs surrender: Don McCullen for Camera Press—Pix
Dead Jordanian: David Newell Smith for Camera Press—Pix
Israeli soldier questions an Arab: Don McCullen for Camera Press—Pix
Israeli soldiers in Bethlehem: David Newell Smith for Camera Press—Pix
Jordanian dead in the wake of battle: David Newell Smith for Camera Press—Pix
Victorious Israelis on way to Bethlehem: David Newell Smith for Camera Press—Pix
Crippled Israeli tank near Garden of Gethsemane: Werner Braun for Camera Press—Pix
In conquered Jerusalem: Werner Braun for Camera Press—Pix
Interrogating captured Egyptian: © Newsphot, Ltd.—Pictorial Parade
Egyptian war dead: London Daily Express
Captured Egyptians under guard: (Credit withheld)
War's aftermath in old Jerusalem: Don McCullen for Camera Press—Pix
General Dayan in Bethlehem: Central Press
Israelis with captured flag: London Daily Express
Israeli soldiers and civilians at the Wailing Wall: Werner Braun for Camera Press—Pix
A young soldier prays: Werner Braun for Camera Press—Pix
Israeli troops at Suez Canal: Gamma-Pix
Men and women, Israeli troops celebrate: London Daily Express
In old Jerusalem at last: © Newsphot, Ltd.—Pictorial Parade

143

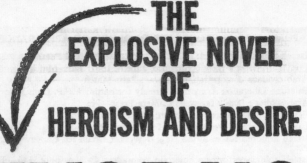

THE EXPLOSIVE NOVEL OF HEROISM AND DESIRE

EXODUS

by
LEON URIS
author of
BATTLE CRY

COMPLETE AND UNABRIDGED
ONLY 95¢

ON SALE WHEREVER
PAPERBACK BOOKS
ARE SOLD

A BANTAM 🐓 BOOK